Cambridge Elements ☰

Elements in Publishing and Book Culture
edited by
Samantha Rayner
University College London
Leah Tether
University of Bristol

WRITING BESTSELLERS

Love, Money, and Creative Practice

Kim Wilkins
University of Queensland

Lisa Bennett
Flinders University

CAMBRIDGE
UNIVERSITY PRESS

CAMBRIDGE
UNIVERSITY PRESS

University Printing House, Cambridge CB2 8BS, United Kingdom

One Liberty Plaza, 20th Floor, New York, NY 10006, USA

477 Williamstown Road, Port Melbourne, VIC 3207, Australia

314–321, 3rd Floor, Plot 3, Splendor Forum, Jasola District Centre,
New Delhi – 110025, India

103 Penang Road, #05–06/07, Visioncrest Commercial, Singapore 238467

Cambridge University Press is part of the University of Cambridge.

It furthers the University's mission by disseminating knowledge in the pursuit of
education, learning, and research at the highest international levels of excellence.

www.cambridge.org
Information on this title: www.cambridge.org/9781108725637
DOI: 10.1017/9781108663724

First published 2021

A catalogue record for this publication is available from the British Library.

ISBN 978-1-108-72563-7 Paperback
ISSN 2514-8524 (online)
ISSN 2514-8516 (print)

Writing Bestsellers

Love, Money, and Creative Practice

Elements in Publishing and Book Culture

DOI: 10.1017/9781108663724

First published online: September 2021

Kim Wilkins

University of Queensland

Lisa Bennett

Flinders University

Author for correspondence: Kim Wilkins, k.wilkins@uq.edu.au

ABSTRACT: While the term 'bestseller' explicitly relates books to sales, commercially successful books are also products of individual creative work. This Element presents a new perspective on the relationship between art and the market, with particular reference to bestselling writers and books. We examine some existing perspectives on art's relationship to the marketplace to trouble persistent binaries that see the two in opposition; we break down the monolith of the marketplace by thinking of it as made up of a range of invested, non-hostile participants such as publishing personnel and readers; we articulate the material dimensions of creative writing in the industry through the words of bestselling writers themselves; and we examine how the existence of bestselling books and writers in the world of letters bears enormous influence on the industry, and on the practice of other writers.

This Element also has a video abstract: www.cambridge.org/ writingbestsellers

KEYWORDS: bestsellers, creativity, writing, publishing, mutualism

ISBNs: 9781108725637 (PB), 9781108663724 (OC)

ISSNs: 2514-8524 (online), 2514-8516 (print)

Contents

Introduction

James Patterson writes books. So does Nora Roberts. Danielle Steel writes them on an old typewriter; George R. R. Martin uses a DOS-based word-processing application called Wordstar. Each of them, along with every other bestselling writer on Forbes' lists, is a flesh-and-blood human located within a specific set of social and material relations, engaged in the mental and physical labour of getting ideas out of their imaginations and onto a page. While the term 'bestseller' explicitly relates books to sales, commercially successful books are also products of individual creative work: that is, 'bestsellers' are people as much as products. Our interest lies in the material conditions of writers and their creative writing, and specifically the influence of the market on the creation of new works. This Element therefore presents a new perspective on the relationship between art and the market, with particular reference to bestselling writers and books.

The view that art (conceived broadly) and commerce are uncomfortably related is a widely held one. According to A. O. Scott (2014: 1) 'There are few modern relationships as fraught as the one between art and money', and Claire Squires (2007: 41) argues that this is 'the central tension of the publishing industry'. Viviana Zelizer (2005) coined the term 'hostile worlds' to describe a view that advocates a division between sacred/intimate and profane/instrumental spheres because, essentially, money can contaminate, trivialise, and/or devalue the meaning of private pleasures. Building on Zelizer's work, Olav Velthuis writes at length about the 'hostile worlds' view and 'the detrimental effects of the confrontation between the logic of the arts and the logic of capitalist markets' (2007: 24). Coslor's ethnographic study of the visual art world suggests this view of the 'corrupting' influence of money is a 'legacy of Romantic sentiments' and shows that while nominally art historians agree that the view is 'simplistic and outdated', it is still evident in attitudes about how art is compared and priced for consumption (2010: 213–14). Tense, fraught, hostile, corrupting. These are negative evaluations of an enduring cultural relation: 'What strip-mining is to nature, the art market has become to culture' (Hughes, cited in Velthuis 2007: 25). But what if we put aside for a while the notion that art is delicate or corruptible or vulnerable to strip-mining? What if we imagine it is not only robust enough to withstand commercial pressure, but that it also has the potential to adapt and be energised by it, or even to shape commercial processes?

In Australia, where we live, bushfires engulf eucalypt forests every year. But after a fire, eucalypt forests thrive. And it isn't simply that the trees have adapted to fiery conditions; they are an active participant in those conditions, with their papery bark, crackling leaf fall, and combustible oil. When a conflagration roars through the forest, it looks to the casual observer like annihilation. Fire is ferocious, powerful, difficult to reckon with. Yet, soon enough thick green shoots appear on the black trunks and the understory bristles with saplings. Fire changes the forest, but that change is not wholly (or even necessarily) negative. Could art works – in this case, stories – be similarly resilient, working with the forces of the market rather than being subject to the market's predation?

This question is a provocation rather than a hypothesis, because clearly bushfires wreak devastation on weaker species as well. But it is a metaphor that we, as storytellers, hope to seize your attention with, as well as a leitmotif we can return to throughout this Element. The language of biology and the natural world is often used metaphorically to describe aspects of the publishing industry. Both in scholarship and in the grey literature, it is not uncommon to see mention of ecosystems, DNA, adaptation, evolution, webs, fields, fishing, buzz, and so on. Staying within this well-developed metaphorical framework, we propose that the relationship between creative practice and the publishing industry can be described as symbiotic. However, there are many types of symbiosis. Parasitism is, after all, a type of symbiosis, and parasitism as a metaphor aligns with the traditionally held views that this Element hopes to disrupt. Instead, we argue that the symbiosis is of the 'mutual obligate' variety. According to Bronstein (2015: 7), obligate symbiosis is a mutually beneficial relationship wherein one organism cannot survive without the other. Creative writers, in order to reach an audience, need the existing infrastructure of traditional publishing or the emerging infrastructure of self-publishing. Publishers cannot ply their trade without content, and content is provided by writers. Moreover, Bronstein notes that in all cases of mutual obligate symbiosis, the species involved have a 'long coevolutionary history' (2015: 7). Again, this metaphor holds for the relationship between writers and publishing, whose roles have developed alongside each other, emerging through the history of challenges and opportunities that have arisen since mass print culture developed in the nineteenth century.

This Element investigates writers' resilience within the market. It presents a nuanced and evidence-based investigation of the relationship between creative practice and commerce. Bestsellers are, in their name, explicitly associated with the marketplace. But what is their relationship to art? And how is that art shaped by and able to shape commercial concerns? The obligate symbiosis view of writing and publishing sees the relationship as a long-standing two-way exchange, which has changed and will continue to change over time, and understands that knowledge of the conditions of the exchange are vital to survival for both organisms. The health of one affects the other; the energy of one powers the other; the concerns of one are the concerns of the other. Writers and publishers sink or swim together.

We are not, however, blind to the power differences between multinational media corporations and individual writers. At the time of writing this Element, we have just watched Penguin Random House absorb Simon & Schuster, effectively leaving us with a 'big four' dominated marketplace; but, in light of this merger, it very much seems the 'big x' paradigm may be displaced in a changed publishing environment with the 'monstrous two': Penguin Random House and Amazon, with all bets off over which company – indeed, which publishing model – will be left standing ten years from now.[1] Nonetheless, within this arena of corporate behemoths, content of all kinds is still required. Writers provide content. Writers who provide bestselling content gain power. To extend the biological metaphor, we might think of bestselling writers as the fittest to survive, the ones who can adapt to tough conditions, ensuring the fate of the species even as individuals falter. It may not be the most palatable of metaphors for talking about art, but art is produced within this system. It behoves us all to understand it, rather than look the other way.

---

[1] With thanks to Beth Driscoll, University of Melbourne, for seeding this nightmare scenario into our imaginations.

This Element argues that creativity is thoroughly sociomaterial, and thus bestseller status for an author will affect their creative writing practice; however, this situation does not necessarily indicate a predatory relationship with the publishing industry sullying pure art. Power and influence can and do travel both ways, especially when the very high sales of bestsellers mean writers can ask for better terms on their contracts, spawn copycat readalike books, and underwrite lower-selling authors' careers. We write back against the tradition of romanticising the solitary creative genius who has no connections to the marketplace, and against the notion that art is *necessarily* vulnerable and precarious, although sometimes it can be. Our research questions are sharpened and made more urgent by the rapid changes in the publishing industry – what we recognise as the post-digital transformation of the sector, which 'by its very speed . . . can be argued to magnify tensions in cultural valuation that would otherwise take a more leisurely time to work themselves out' (Throsby, 2008: np). We approach this argument through a number of methodologies.

First, we have sourced interviews with creative writers who have appeared on the *New York Times* bestseller list: either published interviews in existing outlets or interviews we have conducted ourselves. Limitations existed with the latter approach. Extreme fame makes some authors very difficult to persuade to participate in interviews: in some cases, we dealt with multiple stages of gatekeepers to no avail. Moreover, when a writer reaches a certain level of fame and income, it becomes doubtful their experiences will be extrapolable to others. Can Margaret Atwood, for example, ride the tide of her success without caring too much about what the market wants? The fact that she writes for Wattpad (an online, community-driven storytelling platform) would suggest this is the case. We have supplemented these first-hand accounts with thorough examination of the grey literature, such as trade reports, op-eds, popular media, sales data, and social media (with the usual caveats that platforms for self-promotion are not necessarily the most comprehensive or accurate account of actual writing practice).

Finally, we have also approached this research in a participatory spirit in two key ways. We took part in an online writing 'MasterClass' with James Patterson, which added to our understanding of some motivational and aspirational cogs in the 'bestselling' machine, allowing us to experience them first-hand. We also maintained and reflected on our own writing practices while creating this Element, although those reflections were largely informal, taking the form of casual conversations about work we were doing and the state of the industry we might place those stories in. We are both published writers with multiple global contracts, traditionally published books, and awards, though neither of us have ever appeared on the *NYT* bestseller list (one of us has appeared on the *USA Today* bestseller list, just the once). Our own creative practice and interactions with industry, then, inevitably inform our analysis. Rather than see this as a bias or a weakness, we follow Driscoll and Squires' 'Ullapoolist' spirit in arguing that examinations of the publishing industry should be supplemented beyond 'collecting, counting and modelling' because 'highly abstracted models such as these can close off opportunities for more intimate, involved perspectives on local phenomena' (Driscoll and Squires, 2020: 142). We write this Element as both academics and professional writers, a position that qualifies us to ask and investigate big questions and also, because creative writing is highly individual and personalised, allows us to add nuance to big statements. Our unique situations and experiences within the industry lend this book a perspective that may add value to our findings.

What are Bestsellers?

As Bloom pointed out in 2008, defining a bestseller should be 'simple: the work of fiction sold in the most units . . . to the most people over a set period of time', but, practically speaking, it is a more complex task, affected by things such as what book formats were counted in which territories, over what time period, how fast, how slow, and other considerations. He goes on to note that 'All of this is compounded by an extraordinary lack of evidence' (Bloom 2008: 6), though the volume and variety of publishing and sales data has evolved dramatically in the decade since he wrote these words. Bearing this in mind, this section outlines that evolution and then defines how we will use the term 'bestseller' in this Element.

Bradley locates the arrival of the 'new literary category' of bestseller in the nineteenth century, a result of the rise of the mass market (2002: xiv). Supporting this claim, etymology shows that the term 'bestseller' appears in

English around 1890 (Brohaugh 1997: 264). Throughout the twentieth century, the publishing industry was still seen as an 'old-fashioned gentleman's industry', which made it slow to adopt sales measures, especially as a rationale for acquisitions (Magner 2012: 245). Methods of measuring the success of a book in the marketplace were partly based on sales data (as measured by print runs, orders, and returns, often months later), but also 'partially intuitive' because publishers would not necessarily share raw data. When the Nielsen Company introduced BookScan in 2001, the industry gained a tool of 'unprecedented precision' for measuring sales (Magner 2012: 243). Nonetheless, other ways of compiling bestseller lists persisted, and continue to persist. Grady compares a number of US bestseller lists: *Publishers Weekly*, like many, pulls data from BookScan, even though BookScan does not track e-books; *USA Today* draws figures from the big retailers and a handful of independents; *Indiebound*, the list compiled by the American Booksellers Association, gathers data from hundreds of independent bookstores; Amazon Best Sellers uses the numbers from its own operations (a 65 per cent market share). The method for compiling the *NYT* bestseller list, arguably the list with the greatest name recognition, is 'notoriously cloaked in secrecy', and its methods often speculated on. It appears to be compiled from a mix of print book and e-book retailers, including independents, whose sales may or may not be weighted more heavily than sales from department stores such as Walmart and may or may not count Amazon in-house publications, even if those books are number one on Amazon (Grady 2017). The *New York Times* list also changes its organisation regularly. In 2017, it eliminated a number of lists it had introduced 'as an experiment', including graphic novels and mass market paperbacks (Reid 2017), only to bring those categories back and cut others (the science list and the sports list) in 2019, citing reader interest as the justification (Maher 2019). Nor is the list immune to manipulation: in 2017 Lani Sarem's *Handbook for Mortals* arrived on the *New York Times* list because the author and publisher 'strategically' placed orders for a 'large number of the book from stores that report their sales to the *New York Times*' (Grady 2017).

The Sarem scandal reminds us that bestseller lists do not just count books: they also 'enable certain books to stand out in the marketplace'

(Magner 2012: 246), and drive more sales. As David Barnett observes, 'one 2004 study found that making the NYT bestseller list saw debut authors' sales increase by 57%, while the average for all authors was a 13% boost' (2020). Bestseller lists, especially when compiled with digital point-of-sale data like that collected by BookScan and Amazon, are what Webster calls 'media measures' in that 'they enable media to see users' and, in the case of the publishing industry, adapt their practices to leverage their audience more effectively: for example, through making choices about what to publish in the future (Webster 2014: 17). It has become common practice to 'routinely consider' a writer's previous sales figures before acquiring subsequent manuscripts (Magner 2012: 249). But these media measures, especially those 'offered by recommender systems [that] enable users to see each other', do not simply 'assess popularity, they help create it' (Webster 2014: 18). The data show that 'any book making it to the top of the bestseller list will sustain its sales longer compared to the books that barely make it to the list, indicating that the higher the initial success, the longer it will persist' (Yucesoy et al. 2018: 23). That is, the visibility of the highest-placed books on the list becomes a valuable part of their ongoing marketing. 'Repeat success', in these circumstances, is more likely with fiction because of the ability to serialise characters and storyworlds proven in the market (Yucesoy et al. 2018: 23). Series fiction exploits media measures, giving audiences more of what they have bought in the past. Becoming a visible bestseller creates its own momentum.

We have chosen to investigate the creative practice of writers who have appeared on the *NYT* bestseller list. We made this choice to narrow the parameters of our study, and also because we want to explicitly acknowledge that the highly recognisable epithet '*New York Times* bestseller' has particular salience and agency in the careers of writers: 'it has become the gold standard' (Barnett 2020). Within this subset, we have chosen writers across many genres, age groups, and stages of career. It is important to recognise that creative writing does not sit only inside trade publishing. For example, Anna Todd acquired more than a billion reads of her novel *After* on Wattpad; Naomi Novik's fantasy series *Temeraire* started its life as Patrick O'Brian fan fiction; and Andy Weir's *The Martian* was originally self-published online. However, all of these writers and works appeared on

the *New York Times* list, and it is through that list that they met wider
recognition beyond digital creative communities. We also recognise that
using the *New York Times* list creates a bias towards US authors in the US
market. Global publishing may happen in many corners of the world but, as
writers in the medium-size Anglophone market of Australia, we know that
for English-language publishing the United States (and New York particularly) is a massive lodestone. There would certainly be room for scholarship
that explored the notion of 'bestsellerness' in smaller markets, but that is not
a matter for consideration in this Element.

On a related point, we acknowledge that bestselling writers' fortunes can
vary widely: Yucesoy et al.'s point about position on the bestseller list
affecting ongoing sales demonstrates that clearly. Some bestselling writers
are household names. Others may be a bestseller once then return to the
midlist. Yet others may be a bestseller in their genre (romance, for example), but unknown beyond that particular readership. Varying fortunes lead
to varying opportunities and outcomes for creative practice. The effects,
both for a writer and for the industry, of bestselling success also influence
what gets written next: will a writer turn a bestselling book into a series, or
perhaps abandon a planned series when the first book has low sales? Will
they try to chase a trend (think of all the erotic novels that appeared in
bookstores after the success of *Fifty Shades of Grey*), or will they try to offer
an alternative to a market glutted with erotic novels; teenage saviours of
dystopias; and girls on trains, with dragon tattoos, or gone all together?
Will they steadfastly ignore market trends and seek other ways to support
their writing: graduate scholarships, well-paid spouses, arts grants, and
other forms of twenty-first century patronage? Or will they lead the 'double
life' Lahire writes of (2010), both in and out of the literary field? These are
some of the questions about the influence of the bestseller category on
creative practice that this Element seeks to unpack, and the most recognisable bestseller list is therefore the fittest for this purpose.

The study of bestselling and popular fiction is widely considered to be an
under-served field. This is perhaps becoming less so with the growth in
scholarship in the field of publishing studies, and with a number of edited
book collections published in the last ten years, including *The Cambridge
Companion to Popular Fiction* (Glover and McCracken, 2012), *The*

Bloomsbury Introduction to Popular Fiction (Berberich, 2014), *Twenty-First-Century Popular Fiction* (Murphy and Matterson, 2018), and *New Directions in Popular Fiction: Genre, Distribution, Reproduction* (Gelder, 2016). These books use the key term 'popular fiction', which does not necessarily equate to 'bestsellers', and, as Wilkins, Driscoll and Fletcher (in press) point out, many midlist authors write and publish in popular genres and never become bestsellers (this is, perhaps, the very definition of a midlist writer). However, in the above-mentioned collections, bestsellers as a category and as individual books or series are well accounted for throughout. Texts explicitly about bestsellers include the oft-cited Sutherland's *Bestsellers: Popular Fiction of the 1970s* (1981) and Bloom's *Bestsellers: Popular Fiction since 1900* (2008). Both look backwards to the twentieth century. In 2007, Sutherland published a *Very Short History of Bestsellers*, covering historical through to contemporary Anglophone bestsellers from the UK and the United States. In 2018, Jörg Magenau published *Bücher, die wir lieben – und was sie über uns verraten* ('Books that we love – and what they reveal about us'), an investigation of bestsellers in the German market since 1945, but it is currently not available in English translations. Ever popular, though not scholarly, is Stephen King's part-memoir/part-craft-guide *On Writing* (2000), in which King reflects personally and peripatetically on his own history of grappling with the art-commerce binary. Sustained scholarship about bestsellers or popular fiction more broadly, from the perspective of how texts are created in a publishing ecosystem, is difficult to find.

Scholarship in the field of creative writing studies, though represented by a number of handbooks and established journals, does not grapple directly with bestsellers. Dominique Hecq's collection, *The Creativity Market: Creative Writing in the 21st Century*, includes a range of essays about creative writing and the marketplace, including Jeremy Fisher's analysis of the economic circumstances of authorship in Australia, Graeme Harper's exploration of creative writing outside commercial systems, and Jenn Webb's repudiation of Richard Florida's 'creative class' and her associated reminder that creative writing serves knowledge as much as commerce. Like a great deal of creative writing scholarship, the chapters in Hecq's book attach creative writing to the academy, and thus a different set of economic conventions to our interests; nor does it set out to engage with those books that most tightly intersect with the commercial: bestsellers. In her chapter, Webb suggests 'it may be time for those of us at the autonomous end of the arts spectrum to accept that there is something to be said for the market, or for the idea of market; to examine the extent to which the market may afford fresh ways of thinking about creativity and creative practice' (2012: 45). Here, Webb foreshadows our modus operandi; it is notable that in the nine years since she wrote these words, no other scholar has attempted to take up the challenge in a sustained way.

Each of the chapters that follow touches on different aspects of the writing of bestsellers. Chapter 1 examines some existing perspectives on art's relationship to the marketplace and aims to trouble persistent binaries that see the two in opposition. We break down the monolith of the marketplace by thinking of it as made up of a range of invested, non-hostile participants such as publishing personnel and readers, and trouble Romantic views of art by viewing it as work, as pleasure, and as material relations between people and things. Chapter 2 presents the findings of our interviews, articulating the material dimensions of creative writing in the industry through the words of bestselling writers themselves. Our case studies reveal bestselling writers' lived experiences of creative practice and imaginative habits, both before bestseller status and after, as they approach subsequent writing projects, drawing on interviews with writers such as Andy Weir, Mary Beard, Jeff VanderMeer, and Anne Cleeves. Notably, ideas of art and the market are very much in play in their answers. Personal pleasure in writing may lead to a sense of obligation to audiences, just as success within the constraints of the market may lead to greater freedom of practice. Chapter 3 turns to how the existence of bestselling books and writers in the world of letters exerts enormous influence on the industry, and on the practice of other writers, particularly emerging writers.

Bestselling books create change across the literary and publishing sector. Bestsellers aren't just defined by phenomenal sales figures, they are the stories told about the phenomenon itself. They are also successful (often lucky) artists plying their trade on a professional and global scale, influencing all aspects of how we receive the books they have produced, what the industry is empowered to do because of those books, and how other writers might reshape their own creative practice as they aspire to bestselling success. In this Element, then, we are interested in approaching all sides of this story: its connections and its mutual obligations. We are less interested in 'how to' write a bestseller than in the material conditions and processes of such endeavours: we ask why a bestselling author writes and whether the market has influenced their practice, rather than dwelling on what narrative elements may or may not have enchanted millions of readers worldwide. In sum, our view of this obligate symbiotic relationship is one in which both partners not only thrive, but are inextricably bound together to survive in an era of rapid change.

1 The 'Bestselling Writer' Paradox

The term 'bestselling writer' conflates two different concepts, often seen as in tension with each other. 'Bestselling' explicitly references the marketplace; 'writer' explicitly references creative practice. This chapter takes this potential paradox as its central object of study. We offer a survey of some of the ways writers have been conceptualised, both in terms of what they do (in practice) and who they have come to be (in discourse). The market is never far from these questions: as context, as adversary, as enabler of authorial status. With that in mind, we begin with the persistent art/market binarism, showing how the lived experience of writers consistently undermines any efforts to keep art and the market necessarily opposed to each other. Rather, the relationship between art and the market is often characterised by cooperation; at its nexus, creativity is practised in a material way. Viewing this relationship as one that is not only mutually beneficial to both art and market, but also fundamental to their continued existence, lays the foundations for an expanded definition of bestselling writers: people who create art and also make money.

There are many ways of talking about the art/market binary, but we found it useful to think about other pairs of terms that are often used as substitutes for 'art/market': some that bring more or less specificity to this concept, some that allow more or less rigour, and some that imply more or less moral value. We use many of these terms in this Element, and have plotted several of them below:

art	market
autonomy	commerce
love	money
pleasure	business
creative individual	industrial conglomerate
imagination	rationality
genius	hack

While any of these pairs can be linked with the word 'and' (as we have done in the subtitle of this Element), it is more common to see them set up in conflict with each other. In the Romantic period, this conflict might have been figured as Shelley's nightingale singing for truth and the ages in the 'interfluous wood', and the woodmen who 'vex the nightingales in every dell'. Two centuries later, research into economic aspects of creative work sometimes still purports a 'market-centred reductive view of culture and romanticism of cultural workers' (Lee, 2017: 1078). In this Element, we want to move away from any romanticising of individual creativity (notwithstanding the personal pleasures such ideas may give writers: see Chapter 2); but we also eschew a market-centred perspective wherein creative practice is just another commodity to be traded in a neoliberal system. Like Lee, we want to 'give adequate attention to the location of creativity in the broader ideological battle over the ongoing attempts of mainstream economic thinking to theorise non-economic aspects of human life' (2017: 1081). Our even-handed approach to such a task does not reject economic thinking altogether, but acknowledges its persistent presence while also showing that the art of writing is not destroyed nor even necessarily diminished by economic and industrial concerns. Sometimes, creative writing is energised and given space to develop by the market. Creative autonomy depends on many more things than its relationship to commerce.

Conflict and Cooperation

When we talk about the autonomy of art from the market, we cannot overlook perhaps the most-cited theorist in contemporary publishing studies, Pierre Bourdieu. Bourdieu's relational model of art and the marketplace holds that the literary 'field' is always

> the site of a struggle between the two principles of hierarchization: the heteronomous principle, favourable to those who dominate the field economically and politically (e.g. 'bourgeois art') and the autonomous principle (e.g. 'art for art's sake'), which those of its advocates who are least endowed with specific capital tend to identify with a degree of independence from the economy, seeing temporal failure as a sign of election and success as a sign of compromise. (1993: 40)

In other words, literature will always be pulled towards either economic capital or symbolic capital, with those who have the least symbolic but the most economic capital (such as the bestselling writers we discuss here) being seen as the least able to resist the 'external demands' of the publishing industry (1993: 41). Gelder shows how Bourdieu's distinction between autonomous and heteronomous has lingered around the distinction between literary fiction (or capital 'L' literature) and popular fiction (including bestsellers): the discourse around Literature cleaving to authorial 'individuality, origin and essence', in comparison to the discourse of 'industry' in both the sense of economic institutions and 'sheer hard work' that surrounds the creation of bestsellers (2004: 13–15). These categories are defined in opposition to each other, just as the autonomous and the heteronomous are polar opposites, making conflict the animating force in Bourdieu's conceptualisation of art's production.

By contrast, Howard S. Becker's conceptualisation of the production of art is grounded in a theory of cooperation rather than conflict: works of creative writing, in Becker's view, are 'not the products of individual makers, 'artists' who possess a rare and special gift. They are, rather, joint products of all the people who cooperate via an art world's characteristic conventions to bring works like that into existence' (Becker, 1982: 35). Becker's is a sociology of art, which suggests that even though an individual writer may write the story and have their name attached to it, this writer is nonetheless part of a cooperative network (from critique partners and editors to book designers and delivery drivers) who bring the work into being, and without whom the work would be different. In such a view, the industry personnel are simply nodes among many other nodes in the 'network of cooperative links' that make up an art world (1982: 34–35). Becker admits that art world conventions 'place strong constraints on the artist. They are particularly constraining because they do not exist in isolation, but come in complexly interdependent systems, so that one small change may require a variety of other changes.' However, these constraints do not represent an 'inviolate set of rules' (1982: 31); rather, they are decided collectively for the purposes of both 'making sense of the work', and 'easy and efficient coordination of activity' (1982: 30). Working in the conventional ways agreed upon by the art world therefore both affords and limits certain artistic choices.

Unlike Bourdieu, Becker shows no interest in the struggle around symbolic capital, looking instead for patterns and conventions of cooperation around art – what we might think of as its social and material relations. All artworks, Becker explains, are subject to this logic, 'except for the totally individualistic and therefore unintelligible works' (1982: 14). Without questions of literary value to grapple with or resolve (as they are, in our view, both unresolvable and profoundly uninteresting), Becker opens the floor for questions we *can* answer around the social and material circumstances of creative practice, questions that are critically interesting in our understanding of book culture. For us, the shared and pleasurable work of creating books and stories is central in this regard. Work requires not only inspiration but practice, and practice allows us to reframe creativity (a slippery, slippery term) in a tangible way as creative practice (that is, something that people do).

Creativity and Creative Practice

Keith Sawyer shows how, over time, two main ideas about creativity have been promulgated by culture: creativity as a product of the rational mind, and creativity as a product of Romantic intuition: 'Rationalism is the belief that creativity is generated by the conscious, deliberating, intelligent, rational mind; Romanticism is the belief that creativity bubbles up from an irrational unconscious, and that rational deliberation interferes with the creative process' (2006: 15). The view of the creative artist as somebody outside social structures and operating on inspiration is fairly recent in the history of Western thought, with a provenance in the early nineteenth century (2006: 12–13). In fact, the upheaval of print culture in the nineteenth century contributed greatly to the rise of the Romantic ideal of the autonomous genius. As Raymond Williams argues, the mass production and circulation of books in the Romantic period meant that literature became more visibly subject to the laws of the market, and beholden to the tastes of an anonymous and multiple 'public' who were imagined to exert populist demands on writers (1983: 32).

These factors generated a necessity for artists to see themselves as special and above such fickleness: 'the idea of the independent creative writer, the autonomous genius, was becoming a kind of rule' (Williams, 1983: 32). These and other nineteenth-century writers, especially novelists, were the first to 'experience the full industrialisation of literary production, and they stood at the centre of a sustained debate over the cultural transformations brought about by mechanical production, new techniques of distribution and circulation, and, above all, the staggering growth of reading audiences' (Bradley 2002: xi). Bradley links many writerly anxieties about 'the exponential expansion of the literary industry' to a fear of a more 'democratic (or, as some writers feared, anarchic) access to literary culture', which suggests that a celebration of art for art's sake, in Bourdieusian terms, would be 'enabled by a staged rejection of the growing audience' (Bradley 2002: xi–xii). As Mark Banks points out, then, the Romantic view of the writer 'as the antithesis to the rational and calculative subject of the modern age' was paradoxically 'a product of the very commercial society from which it claimed to stand apart' (2010: 253). Moreover, the rapid commercialisation of books became 'associated with a feminised mass culture', leading to a long history of women being associated with 'marginalised, less legitimate literature' as readers (Driscoll, 2008: 141), and, we would argue, as writers. It is important to keep in mind that the view of what constitutes a valuable creative writer has always been subject to the social and cultural circumstances in which they write, especially with regards to contemporary industrial conventions; and that market appeal can be too easily dismissed as being about money, rather than genuine (and democratic) readerly engagement, and genuine writerly pleasure.

The dominant view of creativity, widely held in Western popular culture, still cleaves strongly to the figure of the Romantic artist, so much so that when artists are asked about their creativity, they 'repeat creativity myths, even though scientific studies of those same individuals later find that it didn't actually happen that way' (Sawyer, 2006: 18). Twenty-first-century Western culture still has a great deal invested in a view of creativity that eschews the rational, including rational negotiations with the demands of industry. As Becker points out, 'if the idea of gift or talent implies the notion of spontaneous expression or sublime inspiration (as it does for many), the businesslike work habits of many artists create an incongruity' (Becker, 1982: 18), and this uneasiness of seeing art associated with the market is often manifested in a diminishment of the creators of such work ('only an airport novelist'), their popular products ('only women's fiction'), and the consumers who perpetuate its creation ('only a bunch of housewives'). In this uneasy view, the publishers that distribute these books can also be villainised: they take advantage of impoverished writers, growing fat on mass-produced goods, no matter the subjective value of that work.

In distinct contrast to the figure of the Romantic artist is Richard Florida's conceptualisation of the 'creative class' (2002): these are people who work in creative industries, and whose flexibility and mobility around work can drive urban change, through their interest both as creators and as consumers of arts and cultural events, food and café experiences, street culture, and ethnic diversity (Florida, 2002: xx). The creative class is thus linked explicitly to economic growth across multiple sectors. Florida's work is emblematic of early twenty-first-century theory that advocated for the value of creative work through appeals to economic benefits (Lee, 2017: 1078), making the arts an easier 'sell' to government and investors. Multiple theorists have criticised this emphasis on the economic benefits of creativity. While Webb notes that the Romantic artist 'existed more in the discourse than in lived experience' (2012: 45), she is not yet ready to assert that creativity can be situated 'firmly in the realm of commodity objects, rather than "advances" in science or arts and rather than exploratory or expressive acts' (2012: 43). Sarah Brouillette, too, is critical of what she calls a 'creative industries imaginary' that presents artists as 'models of contentedly flexible and self-managed workers' (2014: 2). For Brouillette, 'creative-economy discourse dovetails importantly with neoliberalism', something that makes writers' lives precarious and unstable (2014: 7). David Throsby believes creative work is intrinsically important for 'cultural identity, self-recognition and self-esteem', but recognises that such a position 'is likely to be dismissed by economists' (2008: np). In all these critiques, the situation of art and money so close to each other still provokes unease, even after the figure of the Romantic artist, along with his puffy sleeves and lonely farmhouse on the moors, has been (at least nominally) dispensed with. Yet among these theorists there is perhaps not quite such a hard binary perspective. Throsby writes:

> Those in whom the artistic drive is paramount, for whom an artistic vision is all that matters, and who are willing to survive on a minimum of worldly goods, can be interpreted as attaching stronger weight to cultural than to economic value as a motive for production. The opposite will apply to artists interested solely or mainly in the income-producing opportunities of artistic work. The majority of artists and groups will lie somewhere in between, facing a perennial question as to how to trade off pure artistic creativity against hard economic realities (2008: np).

Throsby is right to point out that the 'majority' of writers lie 'somewhere in between' hustling for money and seeking free expression. Our focus, however, is not on the value of either position; rather, it is on how that 'perennial question' of art versus commerce constitutes a materially and socially productive force in creative practice. Rather than suggesting that the system of literary value production boils down to a single tension or struggle between the forces of corporate power and those of autonomous aesthetic judgement, these two types of capital are often, if not always, dynamically and productively in flux (English and Frow, 2006: 53).

Our understanding of creativity is informed by the discipline of social psychology. The long history of psychology's attempts to understand creativity is not relevant here, save to note that in the last thirty years, 'the science of creativity [has] converged to the sociocultural approach, an interdisciplinary approach that explains creative people and their social and cultural contexts ... networks of support, education, cultural background', and so on (Sawyer, 2006: 4). Contemporary creativity theory shows an intense interest in the interactions between creative individuals and their sociomaterial context. The work of Lene Tanggaard and Vlad Glăveanu in particular dislodges creativity from inside the individual and distributes it across interactions between people, and between people and things. Glăveanu's argument is against 'individualism, not the individual. The mind is still a locus of creativity but never in isolation' (2014: 9). Rather, it is the 'characteristics of people's work in creative environments, creative associations, and therefore also material contexts, in which creativity acquires meaning' (Tanggaard,

2012: 22). For Tanggaard, 'contact with or resistance' to sociomaterial conditions is generative of creative outcomes: 'creativity is fundamentally relational' (2012: 25). This stance 'represents a very real break with the individualized conception that creativity originates from intellectual, cognitive achievements or from individual emotional sources' (2012: 24). In fact, such a concept of creativity, while it would 'not reject that creativity is a higher order thinking process', does nonetheless 'reject the idea that such processes are radically cut off from more mundane and everyday cognition' (2012: 23). This last point is important, not because it sees everybody as potentially or necessarily equally creative, but because both 'ordinary' (i.e. commonplace) and 'extraordinary' (i.e. culturally celebrated) creativity share the similar logic that 'they are brought together by a key characteristic: creative action is distributed between multiple actors, creations, places and times' (Glăveanu, 2014: 2). This means that identifying and examining the affordances and limitations of the publishing industry for creative practice can help us 'consider the action potentials embedded within the environment and available to creators for use or change . . . and thus, ultimately, to reconceptualise agency and intentionality' (Glăveanu, 2014: 61).

When we reconceptualise artistic agency within the economic frame, we can enact a perspective shift that allows for the obligate mutualism of writing and the book market. We borrow here from Mark Banks's theory of 'negotiated autonomy'. As Banks points out, there is no disagreement that commercial bodies such as publishers have 'monetised art and exploited artists', but this is not the end of the story: on the one hand, 'artists needed the market to circulate their otherwise invisible works to provide a means of subsistence' (2010: 253); on the other hand, 'capital has no particular interest in fully divesting cultural workers of their autonomy for to do so would undermine the very basis of the value generated in cultural production' (2010: 260). Negotiated autonomy is all about 'seeking opportunities for meaningful self-expression within [capitalism's] limits' (2010: 262). It is important that we remember that, even though the label 'bestseller' describes a book's relationship to sales, these books were written by people, often with deep and affective attachments to the work, and who devotedly ply a route within the established waters of the commercial publishing industry.

So how might this notion of the materiality of creative practice marry up with Bourdieu's field theory? How might we conceptualise the model of a struggle between autonomous and heteronomous forces as encompassing some of that lived experience of creative practice? Bernard Lahire observes that Bourdieu's notion of autonomy in the literary field is modelled on other disciplines such as science, where the path from training to full-time employment is more clearly delineated; by contrast, those engaged in the literary field are often linked to it 'only in a secondary fashion, objectively speaking, even if some consider their connection to this world to be their principal connection' (Lahire, 2010: 443). Bourdieu's model may be suited to study 'the position and differentiated value of works and the publishing houses supporting them', but it is less effective in analysing 'the producers of works and their conditions of production' (2010: 444). That is, while Bourdieu accounts for power structures in the field, he doesn't really account for writers as individuals:

> by disregarding writers as individuals, we nonetheless pass over many central facts that influence the workings of the literary universe. For example, it seems important to ask to what extent a cultural producer in general (and a writer in particular) is situated inside or outside of the 'game' at a given point in his or her trajectory. Clearly inside the game when he publishes, the writer may leave the game for some amount of time to pursue other activities, before reappearing when a new book is published. (Lahire, 2010: 444)

One of the most significant reasons for being unable to stay entirely within the literary field is its lack of financial rewards. As Lahire points out, Bourdieu's model is based on 'the very atypical figure of the *rentier*', someone who, like Flaubert, 'has the economic resources needed to maintain a purely disinterested relationship to his art, to devote himself to it completely, to refuse to produce purely money-making literature, to delay publication of his work until he deems it worthy of publication, to reject literary fashions, and to despise vulgar or useless journalists and critics' (2010: 448). With the *rentier*, artistic freedom is a by-product of economic freedom, and is thus linked to class and other social determinants.

For most writers, this sort of artistic and economic independence is a fantasy. Without generous patrons, dynastic trust funds, or big lottery wins to fund their artistic practice, most twenty-first-century writers are attached to multiple fields at once: they are perpetually torn between the demands of jobs, families, communities, higher education, and also their creative muses. Lahire calls this 'the double life of writers', a fundamental material condition of creative practice. Material consequences of this double orientation might include the time that earning a living takes from writing time (2010: 448); a 'permanent sense of frustration that comes of not being able to devote oneself to one's art'; difficulty processing the 'discrepancy between an individual's subjective definition of self (as a writer) and a large part of that individual's objective life conditions' (445); and 'tensions or contradictions linked to constant movement between one universe ... and another' (447). We suggest also that being partly outside the field in this way limits access to tacit training in professional knowledge – what Becker calls 'professional culture', which is gathered as writers 'participate in the day-to-day activities of the art world. Only people who participate regularly in those activities, practising professionals (however the particular world circumscribes that group), know that culture' (1982: 59); see our discussion of James Patterson later in the Element for some vivid examples. Lahire, then, categorises the players in the field by the extent of their investment, knowledge, and returns in the game: 'occasional players' (amateurs or dilettantes, with a primary job other than writing), 'fanatical players' (most often employed, sometimes independently wealthy or supported by their family), and, importantly for this Element, 'professional players' (2010: 460). These are the writers who can earn their living from their published work; they exist wholly within the literary field, have expert knowledge in its operations, and this situation affects their creative practice in quantifiable ways, just as much as the other 'players' and their creative practice are affected.

Robert Darnton also situates writers within their particular industrial and economic frameworks. His 'communications circuit' model of book publishing lists the author as just one node in a circuit of industrial, economic, and private activity, alongside 'the publisher ... the printer, the shipper, the bookseller, and the reader' (1982: 67–68). The communications circuit 'transmits messages, transforming them en route' (1982: 67). The process encompasses relations between multiple systems, including 'social, political, and cultural, in the surrounding environment', and, because of the scale of this process, traditional book history has focused on one node of the circuit at a time. Darnton suggests, though, that 'the parts do not take on their full significance unless they are related to the whole' (1982: 67). While the disciplinary norms around literary studies might suggest that analysis of bestsellers can be performed through reading and close textual analysis, a methodology that accounts for the communications circuit encourages us to ask about not only the *what* and *why* of a text, but also the *how*. Such questions of process and practice allow us to dislodge ideas of texts as timeless and ahistorical, and reorient them as products of human labour, caught up in all the investments and compromises characteristic of any human endeavour.

Darnton's model was updated by Ray Murray and Squires for the digital age, showing new intermediaries and changed practices (2012). As they point out, 'authors can now publish, market and distribute their work without the aid of a publisher, and the relationships between readers and other agents are being mediated in new ways' (2012: 4). For example, self-published authors are now able to make a direct link to retailers and distributors; although, again, self-publishing comes with its own set of material and social affordances and limits. Paranormal romance author Amanda Hocking, for instance, sold more than a million self-published books before turning to traditional publishing, citing burn-out from the pressure of publishing her own work. In Hocking's case, 'the activities traditionally undertaken by a publisher became impossible to sustain without a very coordinated provision of freelancers and outsource agencies' (Ray Murray and Squires, 2012: 7). When self-publishing, Hocking may have had the freedom to write whatever she chose, but her bestselling success led to a compromise of her time and mental energy. The writer is part of a larger circuit of activity that makes books available in the world; as such, they are always both constrained and enabled by their economic and industrial circumstances.

Readers and 'the Market'

What becomes very much apparent, as the traditional models of publishing break down, is the multiple roles writers can play on the publishing circuit. They increasingly represent themselves, publish themselves, and so on. Digital and social media may mean they have a direct line to their readers too, and they may belong to reading communities themselves. Indeed, one of the value propositions of platforms such as Bookbub and Goodreads is the opportunity for readers to share recommendations and reviews alongside writers. In our experience, writers are, almost without exception, readers first. In fact, they often expressly position themselves as readers, no more clearly than when they are performing bookish enthusiasm online or in interviews. This is an important fact to remember, because, on a very simple level, the publishing market (where the money comes from) is a collection of readers. This is not to say that readers and writers are 'all the same'. Quite clearly, they have different orientations to the commercial practicalities of industry. Bestselling writers gain their bestselling status from having more readers (a larger market share). Markets, for all that they are interested and complex and governed by processes and mediated by organisations, are made of people.

The relationship between writer and reader is a long-standing one. The industry functions as a way to monetise this relationship, but this does not necessarily diminish the good in the relationship; the relationship also embodies mutual influence. As Squires writes, while a novel may change a reader's life, 'the shifting desires of readers also shapes novels. Some of the characteristics of a given manifestation' of a story might lead to something judged by critics as 'deeply conformist', but this view 'pays no heed to how market conditions change the subtle relationship between what readers want and what the industry produces' (2007: 160).

In his essay on the industry's influence on creative practice, Jeremy Fisher describes the 'strong homogeneity' of bestseller lists (2012: 62). Fisher's subtitle is explicitly binary – 'commercialism versus creativity' (2012: 54) – and this binary language pervades his argument. Success in the marketplace, he notes, pushes writers 'towards what is deemed to be commercially successful, rather than creative' (2012: 62). Terms such as 'versus' and 'rather than' operate as familiar fulcra in the discourse of the relationship between art and business. Fisher argues that writers who depend on publishers to get their work into the world 'rarely have the opportunity to be truly creative in their artistic output', and suggests that 'there is little room [for writers] to operate outside the traditional market-place' (2012: 62). If we see the marketplace as made up of readers, his assertion is in some ways like saying 'there is little room for writers to write things people don't want to read' – to which we would reply: well, of course. If a writer does not seek an audience, if they want to write for themselves or a coterie only, then they need not deal with the publishing industry at all. Fisher's characterisation of the relationship between writers and readers is almost hostile: it cites Australian middlebrow writer Robert Dessaix, who 'once recounted to me how he felt obliged to meet the expectations of his purple-haired female readers "of a certain age", because they were the ones who bought his books and this placed certain constraints on him as a writer' (2012: 57). This quotation typecasts readers as the rapacious market: not quite Annie Wilkes, but nonetheless responsible for loading up the creative individual with obligations and inhibiting a writer from being 'truly creative', a phrase that serves as an example of the casual moral judgements often dropped frictionlessly into debates about art and the market. These judgments fail to consider other nodes in the cooperative networks of publishing, including those with shared investments in a particular kind of work.

Of course, the marketplace is not a pure site of readerly love and nothing else. The mediating structures of traditional publishing hold their sway. It has become commonplace to blame the huge success of certain books on 'marketing', or, in the case of digital publishing, 'algorithms', both of which have become shorthand for suggesting publishers are able to buy market segments with tricksy campaigns. But this view underestimates readers and their agency, and is – to our minds, at least – more than a little offensive to readers, echoing some of the nineteenth-century disdain of democratic reading practice, as suggested by Bradley. This impression, too, may not hold much longer as traditional mediating structures of publishing continue to change over time.

Who are Bestselling Writers?

The conceptual work we have presented above is intended to trouble some of the persistent binaries that exist in both academic and popular thought, and provide some new lenses for researchers to try on when they view book culture and its relationship to creative writing. It also provides some backstory to allow us to define perhaps the most important key term in this Element, which is 'bestselling writer'.

Bestselling writers are *people who write books*, and they do so with intention and agency. The focus on the text in literary studies 'leaves out an essential aspect of literature – its creation – and wilfully reduces the scope of the field, leaving the study of literary creation and production to sociologists' (Berensmeyer, Buelens, and Demoor, 2019: 2). Berensmeyer, Buelens, and Demoor list three dominant conceptions of literary authorship: contextualism (where an author can be linked to their work but also their milieu), expressivism (where an author's intention is valued more highly than the critic's in textual analysis), and institutionalism, which they identify as 'defining literature as a practice with norms and conventions that define what readers and authors are and do' (2019: 5). Our conception of authorship cleaves most closely to the latter – not just because the role of institutions is writ large in bestsellerdom, but also because 'practice' is both a noun and a verb. Writing is a thing that writers do, to make literature happen.

Of course, the question of authorship has a long history in literary studies. A bias towards understanding texts biographically in the nineteenth century led to a rejection of the author and an embrace of the text itself in the early twentieth century, as 'a way to bestow credibility and objectivity on the burgeoning professionalisation of literary criticism' (Stougaard-Nielsen, 2019: 270). From the Modernist aesthetic of the impersonal narrator to the New Critical implied author, this turn away from the author reaches its apotheosis in Roland Barthes' much-cited 1967 essay 'The Death of the Author', a full rejection of the 'Author-God'. Although writers in our acquaintance like to assert, with varying degrees of impatience, that they are most decidedly *not* dead, it is unfair to Barthes to suggest his theory was anything more than an intentional intervention aimed at subverting orthodox thinking about literature, for an audience of intellectuals preoccupied with decentring the subject more broadly in a time of social and political change. Within a decade, feminist critics were keen to return subjectivity to the field, given that the implied author was usually imagined to be male and white (Stougaard-Nielsen, 2019: 282).

Overviews of literature on authorship also conventionally cite Foucault's essay 'What is an Author?', in which he describes what he calls the 'author function'. Foucault concedes the absence of the author in the text, but insists the author exists instead as a 'function of discourse'. That is, the author is a constructed social role or 'ideological product' who, Foucault argues, exists to limit interpretations of a text because of our culture's anxiety around the 'proliferation of significations'. He writes, 'if we are accustomed to presenting the author as a genius, as a perpetual surging of invention, it is because, in reality, we make him function in exactly the opposite fashion' (Foucault, 2002: 21). This idea foreshadows the ways that the machinery of literary production (such as the publishing industry, writers festivals, and so on) may seek to delimit how a particular author is defined for social and cultural reasons. Bradley agrees that authors are 'products of ideology' in the sense that they are products of how they imagine their relationship to the sociomaterial conditions of their lives; however, they are also 'individual human agents who set pen to paper to make a living'. In other words, authorship is 'the imagined relationship of writers to the conditions of production and circulation in which they worked' (Bradley 2002: x), but it is also a result of real work. Although the terms 'author' and 'writer' are broadly used interchangeably (and we use both here), we do prefer 'writer'. It reminds us that somebody picked up a pen or dusted off a keyboard or stuck it out with dictation software, and filled blank pages with words. For us, this fundamental and material image, of a writer writing – not just a writer *having written* – has its own Romantic appeal. Just as our ten-year-old imaginations were inspired by the idea of Anna Pavlova practising so much her toes bled, or Jim Henson building and improving his puppets for years before dazzling the world with *The Muppet Show* and *The Dark Crystal*, so too does the idea of doing the work, unrelentingly and with passion and purpose, thrill us. Writers write books, and it is both grindingly hard work and more fun than almost anything else. The author function does exist, of course, but there is a real writer in there too.

Bestselling writers are also *people who make money*, both for themselves and for publishers. In fact, in some cases it may be the best-known thing about them: many readers will remember when J. K. Rowling was declared richer than the Queen of England, for example. English and Frow suggest that 'scholarship on literary celebrity would essentially endorse the *Forbes* metric in regarding celebrity as a euphemised or thinly disguised form of money: it is the *personality form* of money, which appears on the field of cultural activity wherever artists have come to be dominated by commerce' (2006: 41). In a projection of the 'money ruins art' proposition, immense literary celebrity may prompt questions such as 'Has their celebrity corroded their talent, ruined them as writers – and perhaps ruined us as readers, as well, focusing our collective attention too much on the lives of the literati and too little on literature itself?' (English and Frow, 2006: 40). Keeping the concepts of money and literary celebrity tied, they argue that 'literary celebrity, as the example of Rowling would seem to make clear ... has more to do with intensified media conglomeration, increasingly sophisticated and conscious brand management, expanding intellectual property rights, and, at the bottom, the massification of capital, than it does with literary practices (reading, writing, criticism) or literary value' (2006: 41). Though as they point out themselves, many brand name authors (e.g. Nora Roberts, John Grisham) lack 'the aura of "personality," possessing no resonance ... hence not functioning as celebrities at all' (2006: 43). Bestselling writers are people who make money, and who may do so to such a level that they are famous for it – so famous for their earnings, in fact, that in some views it becomes difficult to talk about them as artists without aligning them within the market.

When writers make money, it also makes a good media story, which can boost marketing. In her analysis of this notion, Claire Squires engages with Jonathan Coe's suggestion that 'large advances are as much a media phenomenon as a publishing one' and the media is really only interested in stories about literature when there is a large and unexpected advance involved (2007: 36). While Squires disagrees that this is all journalists are interested in, she does write of a 'hierarchy of marketability': some books are very visible in the literary marketplace while others are all but invisible (usually the midlist). 'For the authors high in the hierarchy of marketability, the authorial role is expanded far beyond that of writer of the text', and now also encompasses bookshop events, literary festivals, and promotional tours (Squires, 2007: 37).

Money can change writers' relationship with their work and with publishers. In Chapter 2, we explore in more detail that dynamic with bestselling authors, but it is important to note that sometimes completely unknown debut authors are rewarded with gobsmacking advances, which becomes part of the anticipatory marketing of their books. Despite pre-publication hype, not all of these authors go on to make the bestseller lists. Great expectations place unpublished writers 'under enormous pressure. And if sales are less than hoped, relations between author and publisher can turn sour' (Sullivan, 2015). Emily Gould's notorious essay 'Into the Woods', describes receiving a six-figure advance for a book that went on to sell only 8,000 copies (Gould, 2014: 122). Three years later her total annual income was $7,000: 'During that $7000 year I also routinely read from my work in front of crowds of people, spoke on panels at colleges, and got hit up for advice by young people' whose coffees she would pay for 'to pretend I wasn't poor' (2014: 121). Heather Demetrios tells a similar story: 'I could not believe the figures in my bank account,' she writes. 'I stepped into my dream life: I quit my day job to write full-time, moved to New York City, bought $15 cocktails' (2019). Low sales saw her subsequent advances dropping, long after she had burned through the money by living the 'dream life' in expensive rentals in Brooklyn (Demetrios 2019). In both cases, the lack of sales and subsequent lack of future income was completely surprising to these two writers, as money is so often seen as a stand-in for market success: 'It took me a while to realise that my book had failed. No one ever told me point-blank that it had. It was more like the failure occurred in tiny increments over the course of two years' (Gould, 2014: 122).

The recent practice of trying to manufacture a bestseller through a huge advance to a debut author seems to have been influenced by the success of authors such as Jonathan Safran Foer, whose US$500,000 advance 'served to demonstrate to publishers just how powerful a marketing tool the advance itself could be. The larger the advance, the louder the publisher's declaration that this is the book the house is gambling on this season' (Williams, 2003). One critic dryly notes that this practice is 'almost creepy ... like trading in virgins' (Sullivan 2015). In these cases, the money comes first, and then bestseller status either does or does not eventuate. Either way, as the publishing director at Bloomsbury points out, big publishing needs highly marketable new content to survive: 'The game plan to make your budget, or exceed it, relies on having bestsellers. That's always been the case, but it's the case now more so than ever' (qtd in Deahl, 2014). In short, publishers need bestsellers.

Bestselling writers are, expressly, people who write and people who make money – for themselves and for their publishers. Neither of those things are controversial until they are made to inhabit the same place. It is in these intertwined definitions that the problem of art versus the marketplace is most acute. This chapter has advocated for removing the 'versus' in such a proposition, highlighting the productive and cooperative relationship between writers and the industry that pays them. In so doing, we aim to sidestep some of the implications of moral or intellectual value around whether a work of art is or is not separate from the market. As writers of genre fiction, a subset of literature often assumed to be written simply to please an industry obsessed with reproducible success, we have often been subject to the assumption that what we make is not art, and that our aims are mercenary: we have both been told on more than one occasion that we write to a formula, market to a specific consumer, and do so to make the big bucks. But these assumptions ignore two fundamentally significant elements of writing and being a writer: in our experience, there is no formula that can make writing easy. Creating worlds, nurturing characters, the two-step of frustration and breakthrough – it is a difficult, often long, process. The feeling that there is a point to the struggle – that, while writing, we are making art – is what sustains so many of us. Few writers have the time, stamina, or objectivity to dedicate their creative lives any other way. This does not preclude us thinking about the industry or where our work fits within it, but our relationship to the possibility of economic gain is background noise, not foreground noise. We set out not to write the next *Harry*

Potter, but simply to write. We are, however, two humble midlist writers. The next chapter takes up the lived experience of being a *New York Times* bestselling writer, to show how that oscillation between background and foreground noise plays out in the big arena of multinational, corporate publishing.

2 Behind the Magician's Curtain

Bestselling writers and magicians have a lot in common. Both stand in the spotlight for a while, conjuring wonders out of thin air, drawing on talents that seem to elude the rest of us. The reactions they inspire in audiences are likewise similar: part cynicism, part awe. No matter how we squint, we cannot quite figure out how they did what they just did – but we suspect there is a trick to it, something we might learn, given time and the right tools. We want them to do it again. And again.

The previous chapter aimed to trouble the imagined hard binary of art and the market, arguing that the market is a key sociomaterial context of creative practice. This chapter leans in closer to look at that sociomaterial detail, so often obfuscated by the magician's curtain. It focuses on social and material circumstances of the bestselling writer's creative practice, with regard to how they are positioned in the industry. Using first-hand accounts, we have sought to understand some of the specific dimensions of how artists relate to the pressures of the market: how achieving bestseller status may have affected writing practice and aspirations, and what obligations and freedoms being a bestseller affords.

In seeking answers to these questions, our approach for this chapter was a direct one: we conducted interviews with a modest but indicative number of international writers, at varying stages of their careers, whose works have appeared on the *NYT* bestseller list. Their books span genres and are aimed at various audiences (fiction, non-fiction, adult, Young Adult [YA]). When necessary, we have supplemented responses from our own interviews with those sourced from articles published in industry journals, commercial magazines, cultural commentary sites, newspapers, and author websites.

Before we turn to the writers' words, though, it is worth noting that the process of enlisting bestselling writers to talk to us presented its own learning points. When we embarked on this research, we cast our net high and wide for interview subjects, but many authors proved to be beyond our reach. Of course, in this digital age, email addresses and/or 'contact' forms are readily available on the websites of all bestselling authors; however, these avenues don't necessarily lead directly to the writers themselves – particularly if they are writing YA fiction. Without exception (and quite understandably), any fans, media, or academics interested in speaking to YA authors are either directed to online 'FAQ' pages or instructed to get in touch with literary agents. We did so – many times – and always received a quick, cordial, and professional reply from these liaisons: 'Thank you for thinking of [X], but s/he is not available for interviews at this time.'

When it comes to the publishing industry, different levels of gatekeeping are to be expected; it is not our intent to make an argument out of silence. Even so, these failed attempts and roadblocks have been illuminating for our study and are worth briefly discussing here. Like their YA counterparts, many bestselling authors of books for adult readers provided contact details for literary or publicity agents, publishers, or other rights representatives; several directed readers to their websites' 'FAQ' pages; and a few, to our delight, replied personally to queries we lodged via their 'contact' web-forms. Perhaps unsurprisingly, many of the queries we lodged via these forms disappeared into the ether. However, each time we emailed an author to request an interview, the rejections we received were sent by an agent or personal assistant. And although these rejections varied in length and detail, they all cited similar reasons why their author was unavailable: '[X] is very busy and just doesn't have time for extra interviews'; '[X] is tucked away working on her new novel and isn't able to take on extra commitments at the moment'; '[X]'s schedule is unmanageably crowded right now so she isn't available'; 'Given [X]'s gruelling travel and writing schedule spanning well into next year, he's unable to participate'; '[X] is not adding any interview requests at this time as he has several projects that are demanding his attention', and so on. While writers at all stages of their careers have multiple demands on their time, bestselling authors often have support teams to help keep their schedules (and priorities) straight. Saying no is easier if someone else can do it for you.

The insights gleaned from these replies are perhaps not as rich as those mined from the detailed interviews we explore in this chapter, yet they nevertheless inform our understanding of the connections between creative practice and market forces, and repeat the patterns we've observed in our one-on-one interviews. The mediated rejection messages we received tell us: (a) that bestselling authors are not working on their masterpieces alone in garrets; (b) that they are aware of industry-related responsibilities and engage with media and self-promotion when they can; (c) it should be expected that they are 'very busy'; and (d) this 'busy-ness' is not exclusively related to writing new work. Being a bestseller involves storytelling that extends far beyond the act of putting words on a page. In their polite refusals, delivered by mediators, we come to understand that being a bestselling writer means managing a considered balance in resources, including time.

Write What You Love

Perhaps one of the most common postures critics of bestselling books adopt is to suggest that these books only exist for 'straightforwardly commercial' reasons (Botting, 2012: 163). As we touched on at the end of the previous chapter, bestsellers are seen as 'profit-minded authors' who write to 'a strict formula that unintentionally stifles the writer's creativity and leads to dry, unreadable prose' (Faktorovic, 2014: 2). Thankfully such views are not common in scholarship, though they do remain fairly widespread anecdotally (speaking as two genre writers in the tertiary sector). The bestselling writers we spoke to, however, were keen to talk up their passionate engagement in their writing, implying that this passion meant they did not pay attention to the market: they continue to write 'for the love of it', as always, and any commercial success was a bonus. A closer examination, though, shows that while 'writing for the love of it' might get them to sit at their desks every day, they are indeed mostly experts on the market: its trends, its demands, and its indisputable place as the context in which they write and reach their readers. The influence of their inherent creative pleasure and the influence of external market forces are both felt, though the former is what they are clearly more interested and engaged in talking about.

'Oh, I love doing it,' Ann Cleeves told us of her writing.[2] The English writer of several bestselling crime series (including *Shetland*, *Vera* and, most recently, *Two Rivers*) had been publishing a novel per year in this

[2] All interview quotations are from Cleeves, A. (2019). Personal interview, 18 November.

genre for twenty years before *Raven Black* (2006) became her breakout
book. What has motivated Cleeves to keep writing since then, she
explained, remains the same as always: 'I love it. It's making stuff up, it's
telling stories, it's what we were born to do, I think. That's how we make
sense of the world.' Given the long career Cleeves has made in publishing
detective novels, we asked if this genre in particular motivated her to keep
writing: did she continue to write this type of story because of contractual
obligations or reader expectations?

> Oh, no, I don't think that; that certainly isn't true for me. If
> I wanted to write something different, I would say so. . . .
> I wouldn't sign the contract. Because you're spending . . .
> pretty much a year, nine months, with these characters and
> telling their stories; you have to enjoy it or [there's] absolutely
> no point doing it. For the first twenty years I had absolutely no
> commercial success at all, so I certainly wouldn't have just kept
> writing for any other reason than for the fun and the love of
> it. . . . I don't feel any pressure now because I still write in
> exactly the same way. I don't feel I've got to write
> a bestseller . . . that doesn't come into it in the slightest.

While it is probably disingenuous for Cleeves to say she had 'absolutely
no commercial success at all' – presumably she was selling well enough to
stay in contract – her midlist history would indicate that we can take her at
her word about loving the genre. She has been writing the same kind of
books for decades, and only recently found bestselling success. Cleeves
notes the length of time it takes to write a novel as prohibitive if she were
not passionately engaged in it. Like many writers, she invokes her
characters almost as real people: a year is a long time to spend with people
one does not like.

Similarly, Jeff VanderMeer has been a writer, editor, and literary critic
since the late 1980s, but it wasn't until his *Southern Reach* trilogy of genre-
bending speculative fiction novels was published by Farrar, Straus and
Giroux (FSG) in 2014 that his work achieved mainstream success. All
three books (*Annihilation*, *Authority*, and *Acceptance*) were released within

an eight-month timespan, a rapid-fire approach to publishing that saw the second and third books make the *NYT* bestseller list, and 'goosed up sales for previous volumes' – a move described as FSG editor Sean McDonald's 'Netflix-inspired strategy' (Wappler, 2017). Seven years before committing to write and deliver *Southern Reach* on this 'binge-friendly schedule' (Wappler, 2017), VanderMeer had made the shift from freelance to full-time writer. At all stages of his career, he explained to us, the motivation to keep writing is 'simply that I have a compulsion to write fiction, and the one thing I learnt early on is that I'd be writing fiction, whether it's published or not.'[3]

This compulsion to write does not blind a writer to the market; however, it certainly casts an almost mystical light on their dogged return to the daily grind. An inherent need to keep writing seems beyond rational control; it is a creative pursuit apparently driven by the heart rather than the head. 'I won't be stopped,' Karen Joy Fowler reportedly said to her husband at the beginning of her writing career (Smith, 2004). Like Cleeves and VanderMeer, Fowler had been publishing fiction for decades before *The Jane Austen Book Club* (2004) hit the bestseller list, where it remained for thirteen weeks. When we spoke to Fowler about her writing process, she too explained that 'in terms of my creative process, nothing has changed. I'm still making up a word and then making up a word to follow that and then, another word, and another, until the words "The End". I keep writing because I like doing it. Mostly. Sometimes. Just often enough.'[4] Given the long lead-up to *The Jane Austen Book Club*'s success, we asked if she'd had any inkling while working on it that this book would have such enormous mainstream appeal. 'I never think about how a book might do in the marketplace as I'm writing it,' Fowler replied. 'I think that would sap all the happiness from the world to do so. . . . I figure my job is to write a book, which is simultaneously hard enough and the only fun part. That's all I think about while writing. Plus, the books I personally like best, the

---

[3] All interview quotations are from VanderMeer, J. (2018). Personal interview, 25 September.

[4] All interview quotations are from Fowler, K. J. (2019). Personal interview, 27 October.

ones that land in my heart, are rarely bestsellers.' The absolute language –
'I *never* think about' the marketplace as it 'would sap *all* the happiness' (our
italics) – gives a sense of the strong feelings Fowler has on this topic, and
how she hopes to be perceived. All three of these writers are keen to present
themselves as driven by art, which we do not doubt they are. But where
does the market sit in this narrative of writing for love?

No matter how much writers may attempt to refute the influence of the
market while producing new work, they reveal themselves to be neither
blind nor immune to its expectations. For Leigh Bardugo, the drive to write
'the stories she wanted to write' has served her well. Bardugo, whose books
have been translated into forty-one languages and have sold more than
three million copies in English, instantly topped the *NYT* bestseller list with
her first YA Fantasy novel *Shadow and Bone* (2012); the six subsequent YA
novels she published followed suit. *Six of Crows* (2015) remained on the list
for more than a year, and Bardugo's first novel for adult readers, *Ninth
House* (2019) debuted at #5. Bardugo advises that market awareness should
not 'hinder you. If you have an idea, pursue it. [Think] about things that
make your story a story that only you could tell – those are the things that
will stand out' (Gentry, 2018). Later in the same interview, however,
Bardugo articulates the tension in balancing the compulsion to write with
the desire to get published. For it is one thing for authors to follow their
muse wherever she may lead them – there are no limits on creativity, no
laws preventing people from pursuing whatever ideas they like in their
writing – but in order to publish stories 'that will stand out', writers need to
know what they are standing out from. 'So you have to know what's selling,
what isn't selling anymore, what people are fatigued by. But that doesn't
mean you can say, "Oh, well, I [can't write that ever]". . . . Be aware of the
market, but really, being aware of the market is just one part of being
a storyteller and thinking about craft' (Gentry, 2018). Bardugo, like many
writers who have experienced success from their debut books onwards, does
not have failures or persistent midlist-ness to round out her understanding
of how publishing works. Bardugo's advice is slightly contradictory pre-
cisely for this reason. On the one hand, she lives by the individualistic 'write
what you love' mantra; on the other, the craft is always and already caught
up in the market. As we explore in our discussion of Patterson's MasterClass

and its 'catch-all' scope, it is publicly impossible for writers to talk about creative practice outside the market: if they were outside the market, they would not have a public to talk to.

In other words, along with typical elements of storytelling – characterisation, plot, setting, structure, and so on – thinking about the story's place in the market has become a fundamental part of the writing process. Bardugo argues that, while drafting new work, '[you have to put] aside ideas about sales or success or ambition' (Gentry, 2018) and just let the ideas flow. This is, of course, sound advice. If there is no manuscript, there can be no sales or 'success' – that is, assuming we interpret success as something commercially quantifiable (the book gets published, reaches readers, and generates revenue for those involved in its production). But even if thinking about the market only enters the writing process in the revision phase, for authors intent on getting their novels out of their hard-drives and into bookstores, this seems to be a necessary step.

This is not to say that bestselling writers possess arcane knowledge about how the publishing industry functions or which works will be the next big thing. We asked Andy Weir if the incredible success of his debut novel *The Martian* (2011/2014),[5] – which appeared on the *NYT* bestseller list for 76 weeks, 19 of which were at #1 – granted him any insights into what stories would work in the current market. 'I don't claim to know the market at all,' he replied.[6] 'I just write what I write and hope it finds an audience.' Weir went on to qualify this response: 'I will say that I appear to have cornered the "hard sci-fi" market. No one else is really doing it. So I guess that's just for me (for now).' Weir is another author who says that a 'love [of] telling stories' continues to fuel his writing, but he was the only one to add: 'Also, you know, money :)' As refreshing as it is frank, Weir's candid response is also significant in that it makes plain an implicit but crucial point in 'thinking about the market' as part of the writing process. After all, markets are not only places where products are transferred from writer to

[5] *The Martian* was originally self-published in 2011; Crown Publishing purchased the rights and re-released it in 2014.

[6] All interview quotations are from Weir, A. (2019). Personal interview, 17 October.

reader; they are places where money changes hands. It too often goes without saying that there is a correlation between 'understanding the market' and 'understanding how to build a sustainable writing career'.

After working as a literary agent, marketing consultant, and senior editor for HarperCollins, Garth Nix has been a full-time writer since 2001. We asked Nix, an Australian author whose children's and YA books, including the bestselling *Old Kingdom* series, have been translated into forty-two languages and have sold in excess of six million copies globally, what motivates him to keep writing, and his response reflects his experience with the business side of publishing. When pursuing new projects, he considers contractual obligations and inspiration: 'except that I pretty much always write what I want to next, regardless of the pressures to do other things'.[7] These pressures can be significant, Nix elaborates, and they include the pressure to recreate 'whatever worked last time . . . particularly when you have a successful series, then publishers always like more of that. . . . But then if the new thing works then they want more of that. It's a very moveable feast.' This lovely metaphor alerts us to one of the things we have observed about publishing: it is certainly a feast-or-famine business, but any publisher who believes the feast is always in the same location is practising very poor risk management. Bestselling trends, like feasts, do move. Sometimes slowly (vampires), sometimes terrifyingly quickly (BDSM erotica). Eventually, the market will have supp'd full of any trend.

Mary Beard – internationally acclaimed classicist, Cambridge University professor, and bestselling author of *SPQR: A History of Ancient Rome* (2015) and *Women & Power* (2017) – seemed perplexed that we would even ask if she considered the market when writing: 'It seems to be self-evident that I should be wanting to communicate with a wider audience,' she told us.[8] 'If you want broad support among the public for research in the ancient world to be funded, you have to tell the wider public about it, don't you!' As an academic, it is a fundamental part of Beard's job description to produce research publications. Over the years, her investigations into the classical

---

[7] All interview quotations are from Nix, G. (2018). Personal Interview, 18 October.

[8] All interview quotations are from Beard, M. (2019). Personal interview, 24 October.

world have generated many non-fiction books and articles; a body of work that, were she a less public-minded scholar, might be circulated amongst a relatively small group of peers in the academy and thus earn citations in their research papers, but not attract a more mainstream audience. Her projects, then, are pursued with market intent, given her recognition that the publishing industry is a powerful vehicle for engaging people in discussions about the ancient world and its relevance today. The broader the audience, the better. However, even with her gaze fixed on engaging the public, Beard told us '[t]here has never been a time when market pressure has led me into a project I wouldn't ordinarily have committed to'.

All these authors show keen awareness of the market even as they play down its influence on their work. Rather than trying to separate out art and the market, love and money, we can see that these things overlap in sometimes unpredictable and dynamic ways. Authors need the market to bring their beloved books to readers; the industry needs them to provide content for readers. While the publishing industry generally has more power than individual writers (we suspect the power dynamics may be equal or reversed for some writers), that power imbalance does not extinguish writers' desire to pursue a passion project. Nor does keeping one eye on the money bend writers' projects out of shape. Bestselling authors say, and believe, that they write exactly what they want to write, *and* (not 'but') these writers know that they write within a context replete with market pressures.

Great Expectations

Unpredictability is a key feature of bestselling authors' writing lives. Many bestselling authors had no inkling or expectation of the huge success they have achieved, nor had they engineered particular practices to ensure success. Even if they think they know how the industry works based on their previous success, many realise that the market shifts: they are cautiously hopeful for long-term success, but not *sure* of it. Even market-savvy authors do not feel entirely confident that their luck will hold. Their aspirations are always dependent on the unpredictability of the market.

Bestselling success often depends on timing. Jörg Magenau speculates: 'To be successful, the book needs a public that sees it as relevant; it needs to connect to current cultural debates, the hot topics of the present', though, as he acknowledges, it is not possible to plan around that timing (2018). Publishing schedules, often organised two or three years in advance, dictate when a book reaches audiences and whether its subject matter strikes at the right cultural moment. Perhaps this is why Tomi Adeyemi's first novel draft 'didn't go anywhere' (Canfield, 2018), while her second manuscript – which became *Children of Blood and Bone* (2018), a YA fantasy steeped in the West African folklore of her heritage, and written in response to the police shootings of black Americans – not only led to a bidding war that resulted in a reputed seven-figure advance, it also debuted at #1 on the *NYT* bestseller list and, at the time of writing, has remained on the list for more than two years. In writing *Children of Blood and Bone*, Adeyemi had a clear goal in mind:

> For me, this is how I try to help the world. This is how I can protest and how I can say something. Often problems like racism or police brutality feel so much bigger than one person, and we ask how we can deal with these [issues]. If I write this and I can make people understand, then I feel like I'm doing my part to fight this and I feel like I *can* fight this. (Hentges, 2018: 217)

There were precedents in YA publishing that suggested *Children of Blood and Bone* would be well received. Angie Thomas's first novel, *The Hate U Give*, for instance, which has central themes of racism and police brutality, was also an instant #1 *NYT* bestseller and was on the list for 50 weeks. While Adeyemi suggests she did not know her own book would be so successful ('I didn't expect this response! I didn't even know this kind of response was possible'), she admits that 'I knew *Children of Blood and Bone* had a chance at being a #1 New York Times Best Seller, but I didn't expect it to stay a best seller for [at that point] 88 weeks' (Carpenter, 2019). This belief in the possibility of listing was largely about the timing of the book's publication, as well as its genre, which we will discuss later.

Unlike Adeyemi, many bestselling authors seemed to have no expectation whatsoever of making the *NYT* list, much less reaching #1. In an interview-slash-retrospective of his writing career for *The Guardian*, John Grisham quips: 'My name became a brand and I'd love to say it was the plan from the start . . . [b]ut the only plan was to keep writing books. And I've stuck to that ever since' (Wroe, 2011). The fairly typical experience Grisham had with his first novel, *A Time to Kill* (1989) didn't prepare him for the astounding success of his second book, *The Firm* (1991), which has sold more than seven million copies. *A Time to Kill* took three years to write; another two years passed before it was published in a small print-run of 5,000 copies, and reception of the book was lukewarm (Wroe, 2011). By contrast, *The Firm* 'became popular so fast I was in a daze. It is something you just can't prepare for' (Wroe 2011). *The Firm* remained on the *NYT* bestseller list for 47 weeks; it was the first in an unparalleled streak of bestsellers (from 1994–2000, Grisham had the #1 bestselling book every year) that has continued unabated for two decades, and has led to Grisham being called a 'megabestseller' (Evain, 2004).

Since Grisham's meteoric career as a bestseller predates the boom in digital publishing, it has always been grounded in traditional publishing models. By contrast, other bestsellers, such as Andy Weir and Diana Gabaldon, began posting their work online long before it was picked up by traditional publishers. On the FAQ page of her website, Gabaldon says she didn't know that almost every book in her *Outlander* series (1991–2020) of historical romance novels would be bestsellers – she didn't even expect the first volume to get published: 'I was going to write a book for practice and never show it to anybody' (Gabaldon, 2020). As Gabaldon tells it, *Outlander*'s narrative began as a series of posts on a CompuServe Literary Forum:

> I posted a piece of the book . . . in order to win an argument
> I was having with a man about how it feels to be pregnant.
> A lot of people who'd been following the argument read the
> piece . . . and they all said, 'Hey, this is good! What is it and
> where's some more?' And so I put up more. (Gabaldon, 2020)

Over the course of a year (an astoundingly short amount of time in this industry), Gabaldon had signed with an agent, finished the manuscript, and attracted the interest of three publishers – one of which immediately offered her a contract for a trilogy – 'and *bing!* I was a novelist,' Gabaldon says (2020).

Likewise, Weir found his first audience on the internet and, as he told us, these readers were idiosyncratic:

> When I wrote *The Martian*, it was just one of my stories – a serial that I intended to work on until it was a complete book. I wrote it for my audience – a bunch of nerds who love to see the science and want the math to check out. I never imagined it would have any mainstream appeal at all.
>
> When you get right down to it, *The Martian* is basically a long series of algebra word problems. I totally understand why people like me enjoy it, but I'm still shocked that anyone else did :)

Although Weir admits that he fantasised about having a bestselling book and film one day, he 'never took those fantasies seriously.' Instead, his more modest best-case scenario involved attracting more readers to his website and 'maybe having an active fan forum on the site as well. That sort of thing.'

Jeff VanderMeer was cautiously optimistic that his *Southern Reach* trilogy would be more commercially successful than his previous novels, all of which can be categorised as Weird Fiction, largely because it was more legible as science fiction, an established genre.

> *Annihilation* [the first book in the series] ... is a strange expedition into the wilderness where something has happened and they don't know what, and the government is investigating it. You don't even have to say it's science fiction; [readers] get that construct. So I had an idea it would do better. I did not know it would do this well.

VanderMeer's suspicions that genre plays a significant role in attracting readers is not unfounded. It is clear to the naked eye that bestsellers represent some genres more than others, and that reproducibility is one of the most valuable things genres offer publishers: they know how to jacket and market crime, because there is a long and established history of crime novels. Genre is central to Mark McGurl's essay on the enormous influence Amazon has had on the publishing market, suggesting that the drive towards reproducibility of success means 'one might go as far as to say that fiction in the Age of Amazon *is* genre fiction' (McGurl, 2016: 457). Writers' aspirations are necessarily conditioned by what works and what does not work, and shaped by other factors in the market, such as trends and genres.

Obligation

Becoming a bestselling writer comes with its own sets of pressures. Some of these pressures are internal, perhaps even imagined: fear of failure, a sense of obligation, imagined poor reception. Some are very real, such as disappointing sales and terrible reviews. Whether internal or external, these pressures are part of the material circumstances of a bestseller's experience, and can affect how books are written and how writers and publishers interact.

For some bestselling authors, like Tara Westover, there's the sneaking suspicion that their success was some sort of fluke. Westover's memoir, *Educated*, has sold more than four million copies and has been translated into forty languages; it debuted at #1 on the *NYT* hardcover bestseller list and, at the time of writing, has remained on this list for more than two years. Nevertheless, Westover has described her success as 'an ongoing thing to process' and, despite the memoir's continued critical and popular recognition, almost a year after its publication she mused, 'you still don't know. That could be a blip. You think that it can't sustain' (Reinstein, 2019).

Surprisingly, even the world's most prolific and bestselling author, Danielle Steel, says she is riddled with self-doubt, and also has to force herself to work through the worry:

> The whole time before, I think, 'Oh god, I'm never going to
> be able to do this.' Then when I sit down to do it, I inevitably
> sit there thinking, 'What if I can't do it?' Only in the last 20

pages do I think, 'Oh, I guess I'll be able to finish this.' . . . The good thing about that, I think, is that so long as you have doubt, you really strive. I work so hard to improve every time. To do it better. To be smoother about certain things. To be able to speak to the reader better. When you get to a place where you think, 'Oh I'm so fabulous, I did this so well,' you're screwed. (Nicolaou, 2018)

Steel's language here tells its own story: strive, work, improve, do better. At this stage of her career, Steel could potentially copy and paste Wikipedia entries together and have a bestseller (though perhaps not twice . . .), but she knows the industry and she knows it can be fickle. Steel's implication here is that doubt, especially about whether or not a book will be a success, is productive of good creative practice.

Looking beyond the incredible success of his first book, Andy Weir told us, 'of course I feel pressure. It's awesome to come out of the gate so strong, but it also means that all subsequent books are unlikely to repeat that success. I could write 50 more books in my life, and when I die they'll say "The author of *The Martian* (and some other stuff) died yesterday".' Overall, Weir's response to this pressure seems to be a sanguine one: 'I don't set myself up for disappointment. If people say "Weir's latest book is good. Not as good as The Martian, but still a solid read and I recommend it" I'll consider that a win.'

For some authors, the sense of being scrutinised after bestselling success seriously disrupts the writing process. Writing *The Kitchen God's Wife* (1991), the follow-up to *The Joy Luck Club* (1989), 'didn't come easy' for Amy Tan, who told the *New York Times* how she'd had several false starts with her second novel. She focused too much on perceived flaws in the manuscript; didn't want to be typecast in terms of subject matter; and 'was very much aware of another aspect of success: that the second book will not be as good, or as well received, as the first' (Rothstein, 1991). Like its predecessor, though, *The Kitchen God's Wife* did indeed do well, spending 38 weeks on the *NYT* bestseller list. But the 'sophomore jinx' can strike even established authors. *The Book Thief* (2005) was Markus Zusak's fifth novel – it spent more than 500 weeks on the *NYT* bestseller list, has sold over sixteen million copies, and has been translated into more than forty languages – but, unlike his previous books, the huge success with this one made Zusak feel that 'that the stakes were higher . . . It suddenly meant that everyone was watching' (Elliot, 2018). It took more than thirteen years for Zusak to overcome the self-doubt that saw him struggling through false start after false start, almost pathologically revising and scrapping whole sections of *Bridge of Clay*, failing 'over and over again' while his publishers repeatedly extended the novel's deadline and his fans hounded him for a new book. 'I'm really lucky that it's not part of my make-up to suffer depression,' Zusak said in an interview for *The Sydney Morning Herald*. 'Because if anything was going to take me there, it would have been this' (Elliot, 2018).

For Tomi Adeyemi, the process of writing her second novel after the international success of *Children of Blood and Bone* was 'technically easier' since she had already created the world, the characters, and had set up the conflict at the end of Book One (Niidas Holm, 2019). But, she explains, the writing process was also different the second time around because now she wasn't doing it alone: other people had a vested interest in this sequel:

> With book one, you do it alone and then people get added into the process. But with book two, all these people who got on the boat while you were still in book one, they're there for the start of book two. I think that's a big reason writers struggle so much with book two . . . You have to learn how to balance protecting that space in your head with the assets but also the noise that comes from more voices, and more interest, and different stakes. (Niidas Holm, 2019)

While the first book may have been written with less industry influence, publication (literally, being made public) means that there is more mediation for the second book. Adeyemi figures this as a boat that needs to be balanced, lest it sink; a chorus of voices that need to be parsed, lest they overwhelm the writer. Adeyemi says that she received support in all this from her editor, who she worked closely with in drafting the second book. This close relationship allowed them to talk her through this sort of 'noise' and into a productive space (Niidas Holm, 2019), but of course this is another mediating experience, showing just how much the market can be present in writing after a bestseller. While Adeyemi has provided an imaginative and overwhelming image of a boat with too many on board, the fact that she solved this problem by working with her editor proves that the pressures she felt were not just internal and imagined, but external and quite real. The industry was very involved in the composition of the second book. But, importantly, Adeyemi does not see her one-on-one relationship with her editor as negative at all; rather, it was the factor that made all the difference.

Even with a supportive team of publishers, editors, publicists, and other gatekeepers protecting their authors' interests, the industry makes demands on bestsellers that it does not make on midlist writers. The need to replicate success means more pressure to produce more work more quickly. Andy Weir told us that *The Martian* has allowed him to write full time, which is a significant change, but now he can't 'just work on things when I want and goof off the rest of the time like I did before. *The Martian* took me three years to write. Subsequent books are under contract and I have to get the first draft done in about a year.' Likewise, unlike early in Ann Cleeves' career, when she earned 'very little advance' or, sometimes, was only paid on the manuscript's delivery, being a bestseller has brought with it 'a contract for a book a year'. Many bestselling authors ignore these deadlines, as we will discuss later; nonetheless, it is an extra layer of pressure that did not exist before success.

Publicity, too, creates pressure. Tomi Adeyemi, for instance, has said that 'life was a lot harder' (Niidaros Holm, 2019) while she was writing the sequel to *Children of Blood and Bone* because of the number of promotional events and the amount of publicity she was doing at the same time. Leigh Bardugo makes appearances at major conventions, such as San Diego Comic-Con, because 'engaging with fans in person and online is now a big part of a best-selling YA author's gig' (Ritz, 2015), but some of her writing time is also dedicated to developing her work into other formats, such as a Netflix series:

> I think there is that vision of the writer off in the woods in their cabin. . . . It's actually just a shit ton of meetings and emails and phone calls. So many phone calls. And legal stuff,

copyright stuff, trying to wrangle this thing. . . . So trying to grapple with that, of all these people who are suddenly crowded into your living room, is a challenge. (Enni, 2019)

Press junkets, travel, book tours, film adaptations, and the internet also interrupt Jeff VanderMeer's writing, so he has learnt to build 'a firewall between the two things'. For VanderMeer, this means 'thinking about a novel and writing down little notes' while he's on the road engaging in person with readers, promoting his work, giving public lectures, and responding to interviews with magazines and academics. When he's involved in these non-writing aspects of a writer's life, VanderMeer no longer 'put[s] pressure on [himself] to write actual scenes, which is where I run into trouble'. Instead, when it comes time to sit down and write a new novel, he steps away from these activities and from social media; doing so 'helps a lot'.

In our interview, Ann Cleeves declared 'Book tours! Book tours are something that I think publishers expect. . . . and for me that's the work part of the business.' However, Cleeves also acknowledged the mutually beneficial side to this aspect of writing life. Although 'publishers are quite competitive and the bestseller list matters to them, probably much less to the authors like me', she explained, doing promotional tours is something Cleeves is not only grateful for ('I'm lucky – there are other mid-list authors who are in the same position that I was twenty years ago who'd give their eyeteeth for the opportunity to be taken around and to meet [readers] and sell books in that way'), it is something she is happy to do for her publishing team: 'I've got such a brilliant team . . . why wouldn't I go and support them by going out on the road, staying in quite nice hotels, meeting lovely readers?' This kind of investment on the publishers' part – what Toni Morrison has described as 'a first-rate publishing effort' shown by 'a family of people who were excited by [her book]' (McDowell, 1981) – can be seen as a self-fulfilling prophecy in the industry. Back in the early 1980s, Morrison gave voice to a thought that is still relevant in our online, social mediated world: if a marketing team invests time and resources into a new book, it draws attention that can translate into sales. '"As an editor," [Morrison] said, "I know the difference between just publishing a book and the kind of elegant publishing my book [*Tar Baby*] received"' (McDowell, 1981).

We might be cynical and reduce all of this to a simple phrase: it takes money to make money. Publicity tours, interviews, and social media all provide platforms to raise author profiles and highlight their 'brand' for increasingly wide audiences, but publishers must be careful where they put their money and so are only likely to provide such platforms for bestselling writers. 'Brand' awareness (and reader loyalty) lead to more sales, which perpetuates the cycle we wrote of in the introduction, where bestsellers sell because they are bestsellers. In the course of interviewing bestselling authors for this Element, however, a different theme emerged in response to this question. 'I do think there is a certain amount of hype that carries you through,' Jeff VanderMeer told us; but, on the other hand, 'what helps is that, here in the US ... [publishers are] very much about publishing authors, not books.' This sort of career-sustaining support does not appear to be restricted to North American publishers, as our discussion with Ann Cleeves demonstrates. Just as Cleeves acknowledges her valuable team of publishers and marketers in the UK and the USA, VanderMeer says that producing, publishing, and promoting his novels is 'a team effort where everyone is working in concert'. Ultimately, for VanderMeer, even if one book was a flop 'they would still have published the next book, and they would have published the book after that. They would have had to take a really monumental tanking for them to abandon me, and so I'm very, very lucky to be with a publisher that is like that.' In Australia, Garth Nix has received similar support from his publishers, who are interested in him and his work, however it has manifested. He told us how, generally, 'in the last twenty years I have always had books sold on contract just on the basis of an outline or sometimes not even that, sometimes just 'untold Garth Nix novel', but I haven't always in fact written what I was supposed to write, anyway, and generally speaking I've got away with it.' In other words, what Nix describes here as obligations (book contracts) are sometimes experienced as freedoms.

Freedom

Becoming a bestseller can change the power dynamic between writers and publishers, giving more power to the writer. Writers with established reputations and publishing track records may find it easier to try their luck with new ideas and projects that extend their brand, in a way that midlist writers grinding out biannual paranormal romances may not.

We cannot let it pass that one of the freedoms bestselling authors enjoy is financial. In our interview, Karen Joy Fowler acknowledged that there have 'been definite changes in my life, in terms of money earned and doors opened'. Garth Nix pointed out that, at the very least, bestselling books help 'pay the bills more than [for instance] buy a vineyard!' In their own ways, both Fowler and Nix articulate a difference between types of bestselling writers: those that make a comfortable living versus those whose income bracket has drastically risen. In many cases, writers' gratitude for their success is about financial security, not luxury. Almost a century has passed since Virginia Woolf conveyed the importance of *A Room of One's Own* (1929) for writers (particularly women writers) and this sentiment remains relevant and powerful in today's industry. N. K. Jemisin, *NYT* bestselling speculative fiction author of *The Fifth Season* (2015), *The Stone Sky* (2017), and *The City We Became* (2020), speaks frankly about how 'best-seller life has made it possible to have' a duplex apartment in Brooklyn in which to work instead of functioning as what Khatchadourian has called 'an urban literary nomad' who writes in coffee shops (2020) – although the coffee shop writer also has a story to tell, which we will come back to in Chapter 3.

We wrote above of the differing fortunes of bestselling writers, and note that there are other forms of financial support available to them besides sales. Robert Macfarlane, like Mary Beard, is a *New York Times* bestseller of non-fiction – in his case, books about landscape, the natural world, and language, including *The Old Ways* (2012), *Landmarks* (2015), and *Underland* (2019). A fellow of Emmanuel College, Cambridge, Macfarlane has been described as 'a figurehead for modern, public-facing academia' (Parlett, 2018). Publishing advances and royalties notwithstanding, academics such as Beard and Macfarlane earn salaries that are partially contingent upon their producing publications. To a greater or lesser extent, these salaries afford them time to write as a condition of their employment. 'My books take five, six or seven years to write and tend to become pretty consuming,' Macfarlane said in a profile piece for *The New York Times*. 'They become the ways I organize my time' (Gray, 2019). The security of the university allows a different kind of freedom, quite separate from the pressures of the market. It affords writers like Beard a certain blitheness that freelance or gig-writers don't necessarily share. 'I don't think the success of the previous work matters very much,' Beard told us. 'It just brings more offers that I turn down!'

Patronage of some sort may play a role in launching writers beyond 'published' to 'bestseller' status, whether this takes the form of a creative arts grants, employment in a related field (e.g. academia, film and media, advertising), or support from spouses or partners. In a recent *Irish Times* article, Claire Hennessey explores the 'multi-hyphenate' careers of many published authors: writers who have not only had many books published, but whose works have achieved critical acclaim, earned awards, and so on – but whose writing alone cannot sustain them financially. Many midlist writers supplement their publication income with writing-related engagements (school visits, teaching workshops, speaking events), while some continue to hold regular day jobs (full- or part-time) and cram their writing in wherever it fits. Among many of these authors, there is a perceived correlation between having the time to write and the funds to make this time possible:

> there's definitely an issue around privilege and the better chances of success people who don't need to work a day job have. While nobody is guaranteed success, being able to write more quickly and potentially get more books on the market more quickly, while also having the time to do events, visit schools, etc (and all the hustle getting those gigs entails) to promote those books can definitely be a huge advantage in boosting your writing career. (David Owen, cited in Hennessey, 2018)

And when it comes to writing bestsellers, the above statement certainly rings true: there *does* seem to be an issue around privilege and success, but, as we discuss later, these privileges can be more than simply financial. What is relevant here, though, is that sometimes a form of patronage *perpetuates* bestselling success rather than incites it. Jodi Picoult, whose last eight novels have debuted at #1 on the *NYT* bestseller list, says that her 'husband's choice to stay at home was an amazing gift ... [offering] a freedom and ability to write whenever I liked' (2020). Jeff VanderMeer gives much credit to his wife Ann, who is an award-winning editor in her own right, and who has 'devoted a lot of time' to the development of his career. 'We really are a team,' he told us, 'and she is integral' to his success. For authors such as Beard and Macfarlane, writing works of non-fiction for international audiences comes with the demands – and the support – of the university that employs them. It goes without saying that bestsellers aren't the only writers with supportive people in their lives, but these authors' visible successes may lighten the burden of such support on family members. It is easier for support networks to rationalise the privileging of a writer's creative endeavours over, for example, family and work relationships, when the rewards for doing so (not strictly financial) are already established and tangible.

Freedom also comes from security beyond the growing numbers in a bank account. For Jeff VanderMeer, being a bestseller has been 'very liberating' in many respects: 'There's enough stuff under contract that [my existing books] could all tank but [my career] would still be in a pretty decent place.' In addition, the nature of his career has changed in that he no longer has to 'hustle' for income as much, which includes not editing as many anthologies or freelancing for as many non-fiction pieces 'to make ends meet'. Most significantly, along with the urge to 'want to experiment more', VanderMeer told us that his successes have given him the 'time and space to just do what I want, which is what I've been doing the whole time; it's just not as difficult'. *Time and space to do as I want*: more than anything else, this phrase sums up one of the most valuable privileges that bestselling status can buy.

This freedom is manifested in different ways and, as Weir expressed, it is not universally felt. For some bestselling authors, their success and industry heft allows them to avoid the 'hustle' and simply get on with writing more books. Dean Koontz, for example, mega-bestselling author of more than 100 thrillers that have sold more than 450 million copies worldwide, 'eschews the trappings that accompany such global literary success' (Pierleoni, 2015). Koontz is notoriously reclusive, but at this point his astronomical sales figures simply speak for him while he gets on with writing the next book. Similarly, Danielle Steel calls herself 'a shy person' and she'd 'be very uncomfortable if people made a big fuss over [me]' (Nicolaou, 2018); so, instead of going on book tours (Steel says she's only done two in her long career) or regularly popping up on social media, she spends most of her time writing. Similarly, Haruki Murakami, whose novels (translated into English from Japanese) have topped the *New York Times* hardcover bestseller list, once told *The Paris Review*: 'I'm a loner. I don't like groups, schools, literary circles . . . In Japan, I don't have any writer friends, because I just want to have . . . distance' (quoted in Fujii, 2014). This sort of distance is acceptable for loners and shy people as long as productivity and sales figures are up.

Reputation and past bestselling success, however, also seems to grant some writers even greater permission to be elusive – even 'enigmatic' (Pierleoni describing Koontz, 2015). Big success may also buy a writer the privilege of playing the diva or the hermit. Bestselling authors can behave abominably and still be lauded (we feel that we need not name names); or even take advance money and disappear for years, à la George RR Martin or Patrick Rothfuss (Flood, 2020).

Though it is clear that Markus Zusak's publishers weren't overjoyed at waiting thirteen years for him to deliver *The Bridge of Clay*, they nevertheless stood by him as he struggled through the writing (and almost endless re-writing) of this follow-up to *The Book Thief* (Elliott, 2018). But while Zusak appears to have been in regular contact with his publishers, other authors withdraw completely, only to reappear many years later with a new manuscript and no visible repercussions for their protracted absence. Instead of being seen as bad behaviour, these disappearing and reappearing acts add to the myth of the 'genius author' secretly slaving away on their next masterpiece. Perhaps most famously, in the aftermath of his success with *The Silence of the Lambs* (1981), Thomas Harris signed a multi-million-dollar, two-book deal, then took ten years to deliver the first manuscript. His editor, Carole Baron, said she had been discussing the book with Harris for years, but had 'resisted asking when he was going to finish it' (Smith, 1999). When it finally appeared in Baron's inbox, the novel was 'rushed into print with unusual speed' (Smith, 1999), and within a single day a print-run of 500,000 copies was projected, along with a reprint of 300,000 copies of *The Silence of the Lambs* (Quinn, 1999).

More recently, Susanna Clarke submitted a 'perfectly constructed new novel' to her publishers at Bloomsbury as part of a new two-book deal, sixteen years after the publication of her bestselling debut historical-fantasy, *Jonathan Strange & Mr Norrell* (2004). Instead of being a mark against her, Clarke's 'long hiatus' and the surprise appearance of a new manuscript seem to have worked in her favour: 'There are few moments in an agent's life when something so unexpected and so wonderful pops up in your inbox, you can't quite believe it,' Clarke's agent, Jonny Geller, told *The Bookseller* (Wood, 2019). Hyperbole or not, Bloomsbury seems to agree with Geller: the book, *Piranesi* (2020), was published globally with an 'ambitious and ground-breaking marketing and publicity campaign' (Wood, 2019). Would *Piranesi* have received such a warm welcome if it had not built upon Clarke's past success with Bloomsbury? Editor-in-chief Alexandra Pringle's reaction to Clarke's new novel suggests otherwise: 'Once in a lifetime do you get to publish a book that becomes encoded in the very DNA of who you are as a publisher. For me and for Bloomsbury, that book was *Jonathan Strange & Mr Norrell*: a book that appeared from the ether like an apparition; I had thought it couldn't be equalled.' This is a sentiment Liese Mayer, Bloomsbury's editorial director, echoes: 'More than a decade ago, *Jonathan Strange & Mr Norrell* took the world by storm. It is a profound privilege to publish Susanna's new novel, *Piranesi*, and we couldn't be more excited' (Wood, 2019). The idea of publishing a novel as a 'profound privilege' underscores the change in power dynamics that becomes possible when an author achieves bestseller status. Although both Mayer's and Pringle's reactions to Clarke and her work are highly romanticised, they have become, whether deliberately or not, part of their marketing story.

Implicit in all of the first-hand accounts discussed in this chapter is the authors' recognition, in one way or another, of the market's role in everything: it is the inescapable noise that is both background and foreground in a bestselling writer's life. The industry is their *workplace*. For them, even more so than for new and emerging authors, the term 'publication' implies a public. Although the ways of reaching that public are continuously and rapidly changing, the traditional publishing industry has established a robust mediating infrastructure for finding that audience – both locally and internationally. In terms of quality control (editorial), design and marketing, distribution channels, and, of course, financial remuneration for creative art, big publishers are rarely outclassed by independents, small presses, or self-publishers. With only a few exceptions, bestselling writers rely on this traditional infrastructure to allow them to continue writing the books they love to write, and sharing them with audiences who love to read.

3 Bestselling Writers and Their Influence on Industry

We have so far aimed to trouble the idea that commercial demands necessarily distort (and devalue) individual creative practice, illustrating some of the ways bestselling writers have experienced the influence of industry on their work, both positively and neutrally. But in obligate mutualism, both organisms, by definition, cannot do anything but bear influence on each other; indeed, one relies on the other for survival. Bearing this obligation in mind, this chapter considers how bestselling writers are powerful forces within the publishing industry: from shaping the practices of emerging writers all the way to bankrolling corporate takeovers. In examining the symbiotic art/commerce relationship from this perspective, we aim to demonstrate the interdependence of individual practice and industrial process. Bestselling writers create books, series, and franchises that generate significant wealth for publishers. Those publishers can then go on to invest that wealth, whether in attracting new talent to their imprints or retaining their midlist authors, or in building their corporate assets for greater profit. In this sense, bestsellers help to keep the publishing mill turning, which in turn generates the resources required to cultivate future bestsellers. Beyond this quantifiable financial stimulus, however, lies an equally important but more ephemeral influence on the industry – that is, the crucial role stories *about* bestselling writers plays in inspiring unpublished or emerging writers. Just like the works these writers publish, the stories about their practices and processes circulate widely and can be emulated, sometimes in formal programmes such as writing courses, other times via aspirational vox pop pieces shared on the internet, and so on. Thus, it is not only the books themselves that become famous: narratives about how those books are made; how they are distributed, lauded, or sensationalised; and even how they eventually fall out of favour are part of the bestseller's distinctive wake of influence.

How Bestselling Books Change the Industry

Bestselling books can change the fortunes of publishers. Bloomsbury was a small independent publisher before the success of J. K. Rowling's Harry Potter series, but now they are a 'multimillion-pound business' (Allen,

2008). An injection of money like this makes it possible for a publisher to take chances on different kinds of books and build literary culture. For example, in speaking about its post-Potter offerings, Bloomsbury cited a 'dark horse' in press in the form of Mary Ann Shaffer's *The Guernsey Literary and Potato Peel Pie Society*. This novel was ultimately a bestseller itself, reaching #1 after eleven weeks on the *New York Times* paperback list in 2009 (this, after also listing for several weeks in hardcover format the year before), but was unique enough at first glance to appear risky to a company who had spent the last ten years selling boy wizard adventures.

The success of E. L. James' *Fifty Shades* series also had a noticeable impact on the industry in a range of ways. Random House employees, for example, each received a $5,000 bonus in 2012 (Roose, 2013). In the same year, the US bookseller Barnes and Noble 'attributed its stronger-than-expected second-quarter earnings to the series' megasuccess' (Roose, 2013). Perhaps most significantly, though, the record-breaking economic success of the series is said to have underpinned the merger of Random House and Penguin in 2012 (Deahl, 2012).

The acquisition, marketing, and book design strategies of traditional publishing houses are all affected by bestsellers. The large, multinational publishers are inherently conservative; more often than not, they will acquire subsequent books by familiar authors, since they 'will be working within established parameters: the author and his or her work is known, and hence there are obvious patterns for representing them to consumers' (Squires, 2007: 87). Publishers will also acquire books by other authors that are similar to bestsellers: the so-called 'readalikes'. One need only think of the erotic readalikes that flooded bookstores after the successes of *Fifty Shades of Grey*, or the countless YA vampire novels that were spawned worldwide after Stephanie Meyer's *Twilight* series soared up the bestseller lists and onto the big screen. Marketing, too, is affected by bestsellers, when marketing personnel use what Spencer calls 'carryover': the replication of marketing strategies from comparable books (2017: 432) – that is, the 'obvious patterns' cited by Squires. Moreover, publishers routinely reproduce jacket styles and even titles in their desire to replicate readerships for books like their (and their competitors') bestselling titles. A spate of books with 'girl' in the title followed on from Stieg Larsson's *The Girl with the*

Dragon Tattoo; and the aesthetic feel of *Twilight*'s cover – black background, red image, white writing – became so ubiquitous after the book's success that it was even used on a repackaging of Emily Brontë's *Wuthering Heights*.

But the influence of bestselling books also trickles further down the chain in the sector. Secondhand books are rarely considered when analysing a given title's footprint, because the original sale is usually the only data we can reliably source to inform discussions about the publishing industry. The end point of the publishing circuit is the reader, who purchases the book and presumably reads it, and may even rate it on *Amazon* or *Goodreads*, or post about it on Twitter, Facebook, Instagram, or other, similar platforms. After the huge success of E. L. James' *Fifty Shades* series, an internet meme arose wherein social media users would find large quantities of the books at secondhand sales, then upload a photo of these (sometimes giant) stacks to engage followers. An Oxfam shop in Swansea, Wales, had so many copies it built a fort out of them (Cox, 2016). These images give a sense of the scale of distribution this book enjoyed, while also doubling as a metaphor for mass market publishing – quantity over quality – because readers are assumed to keep 'quality' books. In fact, the joy and shareability of these images is partly due to the cynical humour they arouse about perceived 'trashy' fiction. As one commenter on the Oxfam book fort says, 'I am . . . disproportionately amused by this' (quoted in Cox, 2016). Not that the *Fifty Shades* series could be considered in any way a failure, but the 'fall' of this giant bestseller has wide influence on bookselling and discourse, just as its rise did.

From these examples we can see some of the short- and long-term effects of individual creative works on the shape of industry practices. Another way that bestsellers display their influence is in the intense interest shown in predicting and producing new bestsellers: literary critics, cultural theorists, social psychologists, publishers of 'how-to' guides, and aspiring authors alike have vested interests in looking behind the magician's curtain to see how the bestselling trick was pulled off. In the grand scheme of things, bestsellers are actually rare and not able to be manufactured (because if they were, they would not be rare). Even so, the persistent and widely held belief that bestselling books, fiction in

particular, must be formulaic to pander to the marketplace suggests that
(a) there is in fact a clear-cut method to writing such books; and (b) that
learning and following this recipe will lead to commercial success. At the
same time, however, 'commercial' and 'formulaic' are two of the most
common slights aimed at bestsellers, especially women's fiction such as
romance. For their part, publishers such as Harlequin/Mills & Boon
supply 'guidelines' to each of their imprints, listing the key elements
and word counts required of submissions. This is a way of codifying the
content of genres, yet it is not the same as a formula for success: many
books contain these elements but are not successes. What differentiates
the kinds of popular books that become NYT bestsellers from other
books in the marketplace is, according to *The Bestseller Code: Anatomy
of the Blockbuster Novel*, 'a fine stardust that's apparently just too difficult
to detect' (Archer and Jockers, 2016: 3). Nevertheless, Archer and
Jockers set out to detect that stardust, and hypothesise that bestsellers
'share an uncanny number of latent features' that can be discovered and
presented by a text-mining algorithm (2016: 6). They call this 'a bestseller
code' (2016: 19). Computers, they argue, are vastly superior to literary
critics at detecting these subtle features because 'computers are experts in
pattern recognition, and computers can study patterns at a scale and level
of granularity that no human could ever manage' (2016: 20). With the
help of a digital algorithm, stardust becomes granularity; the Romantic
comes down to earth.

Using their algorithm, Archer and Jockers identify the shared features of
bestsellers under a tight range of categories. *Themes*: only two to three
themes are explored in bestsellers, and at least one of them must be 'about
human closeness and human connection' (2016: 67). *Plot*: bestsellers share
a three-act structure, but it is always manipulated for 'affective response'
(87); that is 'how the author works the scene-by-scene rhythm …
the million-dollar move is in a good, strong, regular beat' (110). *Word
choice and style*: this is not about highly creative prose, but rather 'the most
common and seemingly boring features of an author's prose' – these 'will
tell you with much more statistical accuracy about which writers will sell
and which ones will not than any fine appreciation of their unique metaphors' (2016: 119).

The Bestseller Code does not purport to be able to help writers or publishers produce a bestseller, explicitly stating 'This is not a prescriptive "how to" book and comes attached to no guarantee' (2016: 29). However, the cover features a quote from *The Guardian* suggesting the book 'may revolutionise the publishing industry', and the book does claim 'We think the bestseller-ometer has the potential to change how we write, publish, and read new fiction' (2016: 201). Even the title of the book, *The Bestseller Code*, seems deliberately chosen to evoke the title of one of the most successful bestsellers of the twenty-first century, *The Da Vinci Code*. As with the notion of 'formulaic' fiction, this title also implies that there *is* a secret (as a code is) to writing a bestseller, and therefore a cipher can be found to 'crack' it. The algorithmic aspect – a promise of precision and granularity – is of course only as strong as the humans who chose the selection of books to feed into it. Archer and Jockers claim around 80 per cent accuracy for their 'bestseller-ometer' model's ability to detect if a book was a bestseller or not, after testing a corpus of 5,000 titles (both traditionally published and e-books) which included 500 *New York Times* bestsellers (2016: 25–26). This range of books was 'designed to look like what you'd see if you walked into a Barnes & Noble with a wide selection to choose from' (2016: 8), which of course means the experiment excluded old or out-of-print books, self-published books, small press publications, or unstocked books from the midlist. While on the surface this may seem unimportant – such books are not bestsellers – it is significant: any of these missed volumes may also contain the aforementioned features of bestsellers, and the fact that they are *not* bestsellers troubles the accuracy of the algorithm. That is, for the algorithm to be proven accurate, it would have to demonstrate that everything that is not currently stocked in large chain bookshops *did not* match the code. For a bestseller code to be perfectly accurate, its database would not only have to encompass an impossibly immense sample of books – sourced from different eras, different countries, and different languages – it would also need to be sophisticated enough to detect significant cultural moments, adapt to changes in personal and political taste, and evolve to reflect national and international zeitgeists. Of course, *accuracy* is not really the point of *The Bestseller Code*, and understanding its algorithm cannot actually create bestsellers. Rather, this book taps into and capitalises on our collective desire to know *how the lucky few did it*. What really drives this algorithm is the ur-myth of the bestseller, the story behind and about these people and their wildly popular stories. For it is in these stories about bestsellers that many writers find inspiration, motivation, and even the urge to change their practice.

Emulation: Myths of Creating Bestsellers

The stories of how writers become bestsellers are the stuff of many newspaper column inches and writers blogs. These stories often draw on the same Romantic notions discussed in Chapter 1, in which artist-geniuses are supposed to be removed from the crude demands of the market. In these myths about bestselling authors, inspiration comes from outside conscious thought (Stephen King has revealed in interviews how the situation and characters for his novel *Misery* came to him in a dream) and/or it is enriched by altered states (Lee Child openly admits to writing his bestselling novels while under the influence of marijuana). To write like an established bestseller, one must find a special place to work, far away from the real world and its commonplace intrusions: Ian Fleming famously wrote his James Bond novels at a six-hectare clifftop retreat in Jamaica, the Goldeneye estate. But even starving artists can and should practice their art in penury in order to become enormous successes: Anna Todd, whose father was a murdered drug addict, grew up in a trailer park in Ohio with aspirations 'to become a teacher or a nurse's assistant' (Bosker, 2018), until her Wattpad story *After* turned her into a literary star.

The story of how J. K. Rowling composed *Harry Potter* is perhaps the most famous bestseller origin story of all. In their work on celebrity novelists, English and Frow explore how these novelists' '"real-life" stories have become objects of special fascination and intense scrutiny, effectively dominating the reception of their work', listing Rowling as a key example (2006: 39). Certainly, the image of Rowling, a single mother on welfare, writing in a café, has become almost as famous as the image of Harry Potter climbing on the Hogwarts Express at King's Cross Station. And, like any great story, it can be broken down into its key elements: conflict, setting, and character.

The conflict of the story is in Rowling's battle against the odds. It is, as Shamsian notes, a 'classic rags-to-riches story. Her parents never received a college education, she lived for years with government assistance as a single mother' (2018). At her 2008 Harvard commencement speech, Rowling emphasised her parents' low socioeconomic background: 'my parents, both of whom came from impoverished backgrounds and neither of whom had been to college, took the view that my overactive imagination was an amusing personal quirk that would never pay a mortgage, or secure a pension' (Rowling, 2008). In this version of her life narrative, she pits her risk-averse parents, fearful of intergenerational poverty, against her inherent desire to write, which manifested in childhood (Shamsian, 2018). Rowling did not share her parents' reservations: 'What I feared most for myself ... was not poverty, but failure' (Rowling, 2008). In fact, Rowling publicly embraces her years in uncertain economic circumstances, crediting government welfare as an enabling factor in realising her creative dreams: 'I couldn't have written this book if I hadn't had a few years where I'd been really as poor as it's possible to go in the UK without being homeless. ... We were on welfare ... for a couple of years' (Rowling, quoted in Shamsian, 2018). Recounted in retrospect, after the *Harry Potter* series became a twenty-first-century megaseller, Rowling's experience of being 'as poor as it's possible to go ... without being homeless' reads like the beginning of a familiar fairy tale: we have no fear whatsoever for our protagonist because we know she rules the whole kingdom in the end. And yet this knowledge does nothing to diminish our enjoyment – indeed, our anticipation – of the rest of the narrative. Rowling declares herself to be 'prouder of [her] years as a single mother than of any other part of [her] life' (Rowling, quoted in Shamsian, 2018), and states in her Harvard address that 'climbing out of poverty by your own efforts, that is indeed something on which to pride yourself' (Rowling, 2008). Some have cast doubt on Rowling's story of poverty and lack of privilege: before becoming a single mother, for instance, she studied French and Classics at Exeter University; one of the cafés she wrote in was owned by her brother-in-law; and, according to an impatient *Yorkshire Post* article, she has done nothing to 'dispel the myth that she'd been a penniless, single mother' (KRT, 2002). These critical voices, however, miss the point that a story is more satisfying if the odds to be overcome are high.

Setting also figures strongly in Rowling's story. As already noted, it has become common knowledge that Rowling wrote some of her *Harry Potter* series in a café, though, as with many myths, the specific details are difficult to pin down. *The Sydney Morning Herald* tells us she went to 'Nicolson's cafe, a small, first-floor coffee shop in damp, grey Nicolson Street [Edinburgh] where she sometimes wrote longhand' (KRT, 2002), while *Insider* suggests she 'visited different Edinburgh cafes and hunkered down to write her first novel on a typewriter' (Shamsian, 2018) – though both sources agree that her baby Jessica 'slept in a pram next to her' (Shamsian, 2018), presumably a very sound sleeper if not roused by the sound of a typewriter. Nicolson's café, now renamed Spoon, features a plaque below the window where Rowling once wrote, which reads 'J. K. ROWLING wrote some of the early chapters of HARRY POTTER in the rooms on the First Floor of this building'. More boldly, the Elephant House café, also in Edinburgh, announces over its front door that it is the 'birthplace of Harry Potter'. On its website, the claim is slightly moderated: 'the place of inspiration to writers such as J.K. Rowling, who sat writing much of her early novels in the back room overlooking Edinburgh Castle'. In May 2020, Rowling contradicted the 'birthplace' claim, tweeting 'I'd been writing Potter for several years before I ever set foot in this cafe, so it's not the birthplace, but I *did* write in there so we'll let them off!' She then shared a picture of an ordinary London street corner, flats above and slightly grubby shops below, with the accompanying text: 'This is the true birthplace of Harry Potter, if you define "birthplace" as the spot where I put pen to paper for the first time. I was renting a room in a flat over what was then a sports shop. The first bricks of Hogwarts were laid in a flat in Clapham Junction.'[9] Again, the story is made more compelling both by the elusiveness and the realities of the setting: a dingy flat versus a café with a view of Edinburgh Castle. Rowling herself has said she is 'perennially amused by the idea that Hogwarts was directly inspired by beautiful places I saw or visited because it's so far from the truth' (Rowling, quoted in Lord, 2020); like Harry, she had to escape difficult, mundane circumstances to be transported to magical ones.

---

[9] https://twitter.com/jk_rowling/status/1263439084636319746?lang=en

The final element of the story is the character, but in this context we are not looking at Rowling herself, but at how other, emerging writers may see themselves as potential bestsellers by imagining themselves into similar conflicts and situations. While writing in cafés is nothing new – literary salons in coffee houses have endured since the eighteenth century – a new salience has been brought to the practice by Rowling's fame, spawning countless social media posts of emerging writers at Rowling's cafes, working on laptops or in notebooks (or, in one image we saw, writing a shopping list), and featuring the hashtags #cafewriting and #writingincafes (often alongside the common and patently untrue #amwriting). When David Paul Kirkpatrick, an emerging writer and blogger, posted about his experience of visiting the Elephant House café in Edinburgh, he not only encapsulated the sense of place, he also conveyed the spirit of pilgrimage shared by many new writers like him: those who seek out the haunts of their idols as though *places* can stand in for *people* and, in fostering a communion between them, inspire his own writing practice:

> She had a favourite table. It was by a window that looked out onto Edinburgh Castle. . . . there was a space heater to the left of the window where she could park the stroller so her baby could keep warm during the winter months. . . . Rowling would work there every morning, nursing a single cup of coffee or tea so she could hold on to her writing spot. (2019)

The details make the story: the position of the table and the heater, the single cup of coffee being 'nursed' so Rowling is not kicked out in the cold. Kirkpatrick relates – and perhaps *relates to* – this specifically as Rowling's 'story of hardship'. To start her career as a bestselling author, all Rowling had was 'a coffee shop and an occasional welfare check' (Kirkpatrick, 2019). This is a specific vision of Rowling's winter of obscurity. Focusing on that hardship, the grind, the looming slush pile awaiting her manuscript – while simultaneously knowing that manuscript rises to the top, and beyond – allows unpublished writers to imagine themselves in Rowling's shoes, and perhaps into a similar future.

Kirkpatrick, however, goes on to reflect that he felt he was 'trespassing' at 'that special table': 'This was not my world of writing, it was another's. It was another's story, not my own' (2019). In a moment of self-reflection, Kirkpatrick sees himself from the outside: he is not J. K. Rowling, and nor is anyone else, no matter how much hardship they suffer or how long they go on unpublished, how many rejection letters they rack up. But he continues to use the mythic language of the emerging writer, noting that while bestselling books did not come from sitting at Rowling's table, his epiphany did. 'As I sat at J. K. Rowling's table, I had an epiphany, not only for myself, but an epiphany for all my fellow writers. Yes, sometimes, we see greener grass and read about another author's life and it seems so delicious. But that is not our way' (2019). Kirkpatrick's desire to imagine himself in Rowling's life, and his desire to see himself as forging his own path, both have a mythic quality to them. But rather than suggest that Kirkpatrick needs to face reality, we recognise the pleasure Kirkpatrick takes in these myths about who writers are and what they do. Rowling's story is compelling because it brims with creative mythology, and that has a material effect: writers continue to work in cafes, bloggers continue to have epiphanies, and so on. While myths about creativity can undoubtedly have a counterproductive complexion (we know all too well that waiting for inspiration is one of the best ways to miss a deadline), less is said about how productive inventing and musing on these too-good-to-be-true narratives can be too. Creativity, like dreaming, is something ordinary that seems out of the ordinary. We attach stories to it because it gives us pleasure to do so and this pleasure is not trivial. There can be no doubt that Rowling's bestselling writing has inspired many, many writers. If it takes a little magical thinking and 'rags-to-riches' mythologising to get words on the page, there is likely nothing wrong with that.

Training: Secrets of Writing Bestsellers

Visiting a café where *Harry Potter* was written is one way to emulate bestselling writing. Another, more instrumental approach, is to deliberately set out to learn to write a bestseller. Many books, courses, and blogs make the promise of teaching bestselling writing, despite the fact that their authors are not bestsellers themselves, or can only claim to be so in a circular way: Paula Wynne, for example, the author of *Pimp my Fiction: Write a Bestselling Novel*, claims bestselling status as the 'author of the bestselling *Pimp my Fiction*' (Wynne, 2020). This is not to unfairly target Wynne by any means; an entire cottage industry exists in teaching people how to write bestsellers. But if, as we explored above, there is no bestseller 'code' to be reliably cracked, and if the proponents of 'how-to' books are not writing bestsellers themselves, then surely they must be lacking the requisite knowledge or skillset to pass on to their students. Would it not be better to learn from the bestselling author on the planet? This was probably the rationale behind the American online education company MasterClass's *James Patterson Teaches Writing*. The sedate title of the MasterClass belies its content, which is very much about 'what you'll need to learn to start writing your own best-sellers' (MasterClass, 2019). As Patterson says in their marketing collateral: 'Write a story, not a bunch of pretty sentences. Don't set out to write a thriller, set out to write a #1 thriller!'

Patterson, of all people, should know what goes into a bestseller. At the time of writing, he has had 114 *New York Times* bestsellers, including 67 at #1. What is interesting about the MasterClass model is not that the lessons it provides are exponentially more insightful than texts such as Wynne's. The lessons are, in fact, what one might see at any community writing course: how to plot, how to develop character, how to craft dialogue, and so on. As writers who also teach workshops, we participated in Patterson's MasterClass and discovered that his content bears little difference from what we have taught ourselves. He attributes these *common* elements of craft, however, as the underpinning of his own *unique* success in the marketplace, essentially disconnecting the craft from the desired-for out-come. Rather than teaching writing, Patterson models bestseller-ness, which is ultimately out of reach for most, if not all, participants of his class, considering his *sui generis* status in the industry. The specific fact of his being superstar author James Patterson is both the chief strength and one of the paradoxical weaknesses of the MasterClass.

Patterson is very clear that *he* is the unique value proposition of this course. In his discussion about endings, for instance, he suggests there are no 'rules', but the participant is welcome to 'go to somebody else's class for it' if they believe such rules exist; later, he says 'now here's the real secret, okay, to endings'. Here, Patterson acknowledges there may be 'somebody else' other than him who has bestselling wisdom: but the implication is that *that* person only has rules, whereas Patterson has secrets. As a storyteller, Patterson knows how much more inviting secrets are than rules. In fact, much is made of the 'secrets' that Patterson may be able to teach: 'We're going to talk a lot about if there are secrets to being a bestseller,' he says at one point. This is what the aspiring writer signs up for: insider knowledge that other bestseller-teachers either do not possess or are unwilling to divulge. The captions, worksheets, and handouts that accompany the video modules similarly employ the language of secrets and special knowledge: writers can learn 'James's secret weapon' and gain access to documents he has never shown 'to anyone (not even his publisher) until now'. 'No matter what,' they tell us, 'don't skip this lesson!'

Participants in this workshop may be somewhat disappointed to learn that the biggest 'secret' to Patterson's success is something so ordinary as outlining the plot in advance. 'The most common mistake that most writers make, especially young writers,' Patterson tells us, 'is that *they don't do an outline!*' He shouts this last part with a laugh, hammering home the simplicity of the so-called secret (and, perhaps, of the writers who have nevertheless failed to notice it). This lesson is accompanied by the 27-page outline of his novel *Honeymoon*, along with some broad exercises designed to get writers started on their own outlines. In other words, little about this module is specific: we do not learn any 'secrets' in these exercises. Perhaps this is because, as Patterson later acknowledges, there is no secret: 'ultimately, it's a gut feeling,' he says. 'I don't know if I can teach you about that, so much as make you aware of it.'

From our perspective, this secretless secret is the axle around which the most compelling myth of the bestseller spins; it both drives and perpetuates a desire for the 'how-to' market, propelled forward with such irresistible force that writers and researchers alike cannot help but get swept up in it. This secret is the publishing industry's philosopher's stone: it is the 'x factor' that even a mega-bestseller like Patterson cannot find the right words to articulate. Not that this prevents him from trying. In his MasterClass,

Patterson presents himself as a likeable older friend who simply has more experience in the field than his audience. He speaks directly to the audience in everyday language, cracking jokes and swearing, reinforcing the sense that he's just an Average Joe who got lucky. He encourages writers to become 'so hooked by the idea yourself, as the author, you can't wait to see where it goes', and speaks frankly of the pleasure of writing: 'What, are you fucking nuts? I'm taking the cup of joy every time.' In the lesson on getting published, he offers empathy: 'I know what you're going through' he says, then emphasises the kind of 'persistence' that saw him secure his first book deal. He describes his excitement when visiting Little, Brown after they had made their offer: 'I went there . . . up to their offices and I'm sitting in this room *filled* with all the books they've published . . . There's *Catcher in the Rye* . . . and all this stuff, and the fire's burning in the fireplace; it's real old-time shit, you know . . . And it was the best!' Without the benefit of his ebullient tone, it is hard to fully capture how much Patterson performs his contagious enthusiasm and nerdy bookishness in this story he tells. Calling it a performance is not to accuse him of being disingenuous; his delight is clearly authentic. But Patterson is a storyteller and a marketeer, and he knows how to work a crowd. His observations operate phatically, creating social closeness, suggesting that Patterson, like you, is simply a person passionate about stories and books. This shared affect amplifies the feeling that Patterson is taking writers into his confidence, his inner circle where the special knowledge lies.

However, there are places throughout the MasterClass where this phatic bond slips, and the difference between Patterson (bestselling writer) and audience (emerging writer) becomes starkly apparent. In the very same story, about his first offer for publication, it becomes clear he is speaking of a different era of publishing when the traditional route of agent, editor, publisher was the norm, and the industry was not yet dominated by an ever-shrinking number of multinational conglomerates. His agent fielded four offers within a week of submission, and Patterson, who was the CEO of one of the largest advertising agencies in the world at that time, lived close enough to the publishing centre of New York to be able to visit Little, Brown and sign his contracts in person. So the story of the excited writer, whose persistence lifted him out of the doldrums of rejection, is immediately revealed to be exceptional, and not an experience new writers today can reasonably hope to share.

He shows in many other ways how both his interactions with the market as well as his writing practice are fundamentally unique. For example, unlike other writers, he says he remembers all his good ideas and does not 'wake up in the middle of the night to write notes' though '*you* might want to write stuff down'. He also advises writers to think of their readers as women, because 'women buy 70 per cent of the books', then qualifies this statement with 'women buy 70 per cent of *my* books'. While we are not sure where he draws his data from, it does appear as though Patterson is suggesting that his experience is extrapolable to all writers. The data we have seen about book buying and reading behaviour is certainly more nuanced than a 70/30 split across all genres (see, for example, Nielsen and Statista[10]). On writers block, he suggests writers just 'get it down' like a 'freight train through the first draft', noting that he can do a first draft in a month: 'I'm amazed at how much I do in a short amount of time'. Notwithstanding the issue of his vastly greater experience, which enables him to draft a novel in a month, this quotation also reveals his privilege as somebody who can devote all their time to writing. In fact, the description of his writing process is well beyond the reach of most people. In the MasterClass, Patterson reveals that he writes seven days a week, in the morning after reading the paper; has an assistant who transcribes his hand-written notes onto the computer; walks a golf course for an hour or so in the mornings; then comes back and writes until lunchtime; has lunch with his wife; then comes back and writes some more; and 'I pretty much do that every day'. What are the secrets here? He has no other job to go to (in fact, he does not 'believe people do two things well at one time'); he has access to an assistant and a golf course; and his wife does not have excessive demands on her time, unlike some writers who live off the patronage of their spouses. In this description of his writing process, Patterson does not sell writing advice so much as he sells a fantasy of a bestselling writer's lifestyle.

Nowhere is this selling of a fantasy more apparent than when the course moves away from advice about craft and into advice about the industry. He

---

[10] https://online.nielsenbookscan.net/; www.statista.com/

teaches students not about approaching publishers but about the difference between print, radio, and television advertisements for books they have not even written yet, making points about ad placement and capturing audience attention. This may well be fuelled by his own 'lurid past in advertising', which he admits assists him in marketing his books, but for an unpublished writer, or even a writer with a small-to-medium contract in hand, this content is of questionable educational value. The module he offers on Hollywood is more of the same: at this point, with the aspiring writer yet to have their outline finished let alone their 'freight train' first draft, he turns to nostalgic stories about adaptations of his own novels: how he pitches to movie producers on sets and is offered six-figure deals on the spot. This is rocket-fuel for fantasy, not for improving one's craft. Overall, Patterson's MasterClass demonstrates the double-edged sword of learning how to write a bestseller from an actual bestseller: his experience, by definition, is atypical. Nonetheless, as we noted earlier with respect to *The Bestseller Code*, Patterson's MasterClass does not necessarily exist to actually produce more bestsellers. It is a *product* of bestsellers (Patterson's) and shows both that bestselling writers influence other writers in a multitude of ways, and that bestselling writers can extend their franchises in many ways besides their books. These are examples of the power of bestselling writers to shape the industry that also shapes them.

Throughout this Element, we have argued that bestsellers and the market are two sides of the same coin; however you flip it, heads and tails will revolve around one another, their fortunes rising and falling together. In this chapter, we have explored the idea that although the power structures in publishing may appear monolithic from afar, a closer view shows the many ways that bestselling writers affect the shape and scope of this industry. Bestselling writers, through their work, can change processes within the industry, from acquisition to marketing to bookselling. As public figures who seem to have won the publishing lottery, they have a particular influence on aspiring writers, who hope to emulate their success by learning their secrets and, ideally, repeating their practices. The myths surrounding bestsellers can have material outcomes: more of their books are sold, read, and discussed globally; subsidiary markets (of critics, academics, reviewers, 'how-to' guides) crop up and thrive around them and their works; and their reputations translate into bankable insights, 'secrets' shared with anyone able to invest in their one-on-one MasterClasses. By not only functioning within but also furthering the industrial complex that supports them, bestselling writers demonstrate most acutely that art and the market do not exist in a predator–prey relationship, but in an obligate mutualist symbiosis.

Conclusion

The sepia-toned retrospective narrative James Patterson tells of selling his first book – the condensed struggle to place his manuscript, hardship that is soon overshadowed by an exciting visit to the Big Smoke, where the publishers welcomed him in person to their impressive house – strikes a chord not just because he is an engaging storyteller, but because this story is an effective piece of nostalgia marketing. It is another appealing myth that hearkens back to an era of publishing that many twenty-first-century writers have only encountered secondhand; in books, popular culture, or anecdotes like this one, told by authors whose careers were established before the digital age wrought significant change on the industry and on writers' fortunes. Stories like Patterson's speak of experiences in publishing that few, if any, writers in this cultural moment will likely experience. The days of such face-to-face meetings to sign first contracts (not to mention long promotional tours after the book's release; marketing budgets for midlist authors; or even funded appearances at international book fairs and writers' festivals) are, to a greater or lesser extent, becoming things of the past.

Even so, these stories are significant because they feed the dream-machine that drives this industry. They perhaps overstate the publishers' pandering to their authors, but even in doing so, they point to an idea that is at the core of this Element: without artists there would be no market, and without financial investment in creative practitioners there would be much less art in the world. From the first draft to the final product, a professional writer's process is firmly entrenched within an awareness of, and reliance upon, the industrial complex. This two-way exchange is, we argue, not only beneficial to both sides of the publishing industry – the creative and the commercial – it is central to its existence. Our approach in this book, then, has been to interrogate and add nuance to Romantic constructions of the market as something outside of (and often hostile to) the creation of art, by undertaking an evidence-based investigation of the relationship between creative practice and commerce. Rather than viewing this relationship as a predatory one that ultimately devalues or degrades art, we have instead suggested a shift in focus: one that acknowledges the resilience of art in the market, and, indeed, its power to shape and influence it.

Bestsellers are ideally positioned to illustrate our obligate symbiosis view of creative writing and the industry, and, as Amazon dominates a publishing world that is currently also being inundated with a pandemic-driven demand for books, our investigation into their role in the market-place is particularly relevant. At the time of writing, Penguin Random House is brokering a $3 billion merger with Simon & Schuster, a deal that will 'create a book industry supergiant' designed to level the playing field when bargaining with online retailers like Amazon, but which has caused critics to 'worry that bigger behemoths in publishing [will] wield increasing power over authors' (Carras and Faughnder, 2020). It remains to be seen if and/or how such a merger will affect new authors in an industry that has recently been described as 'more profit focused, consolidated, undifferen-tiated and averse to risk' than ever, and, as we have likewise suggested in this Element, 'increasingly reliant on blockbusters' (Alter, 2020). However, as we have also pointed out, this relationship has traditionally had notable and not necessarily negative effects for new, emerging, and midlist authors. Without the income derived from bestsellers, many publishing houses would not have the capital to take chances on manuscripts by unknown writers.

The material impact of COVID-19 on publishers, printers, and brick-and-mortar retailers in 2020 and 2021 seems to be amplifying the importance of bestsellers in the industry's survival – perhaps to the detriment of midlist or new authors. At a moment when so many people are turning to books for comfort and escape that there is literally not enough paper to keep up with the demand (Alter, 2020), the priority for publishing giants like Penguin Random House is 'getting readers the books they want. And what many of them want are books that other people already bought', which, as Alexandra Alter observes, results in 'an algorithmic marketplace that serves up mostly the hits, driving a cycle so self-fulfilling it's nearly tautological: Best sellers sell the best because they are best sellers' (Alter 2020).

Compounding the sense that publishers are disproportionately con-strained by the whims of the consumer is the fact that, at present, when readers are not adding recent bestsellers to their carts, they are comfort-buying older ones – everything from *The Handmaid's Tale* to *The Very Hungry Caterpillar* – which means that publishers and printers may be investing their time and money into the past, not the future: 'Every dollar ploughed into printing and marketing older titles comes at the expense of discovering and promoting new writers' (Alter, 2020). Whether this pandemic-driven trend is long- or short-lived, its reliance on bestsellers will not necessarily lead to 'a sort of slow stagnation of literary culture' as Alter argues, but will most likely serve to reinforce the status quo. After all, our conception of an obligate symbiosis between writers and publishers is unashamedly, though not blindly, optimistic. Bestsellers are and will remain vital partners in this relationship with the publishing industry. The art they will create is not so much sullied by money, but rather may continue to be made possible because of it. In turn, the income these bestsellers generate will shape the industry, including the possibility of facilitating the art of other creative practitioners. Awareness of the market, its demands and restrictions as well as its advantages, will not stifle artistic impulses – writers will continue to write for the love of it, as always. Meanwhile, the conditions of this symbiotic partnership will (indeed, *must*) evolve, not just to prevent literary stagnation, but to avoid extinction.

Bibliography

Allen, K. (2008). Bloomsbury Confident of Life after Harry Potter. *The Guardian*, 2 April. Available at: www.theguardian.com/books/2008/apr/02/harrypotter.jkjoannekathleenrowling.

Alter, A. (2020). Best Sellers Sell the Best Because They're Best Sellers. *The New York Times*, 19 September. Available at: www.nytimes.com/2020/09/19/books/penguin-random-house-madeline-mcintosh.html.

Archer, J. and Jockers, M. L. (2016). *The Bestseller Code: Anatomy of the Blockbuster Novel*. New York: St Martin's Press.

Banks, M. (2010). Autonomy Guaranteed? Cultural Work and the 'Art-Commerce Relation'. *Journal for Cultural Research*, 14.3, 251–69.

Barnett, David. (2020). An Author Bought His Own Book to Get Higher on Bestseller Lists. Is that Fair? *The Guardian*, 21 July. Available at: www.theguardian.com/books/booksblog/2020/jul/20/an-author-bought-his-own-book-to-get-higher-on-bestseller-lists-is-that-fair.

Becker, H. S. (1982). *Art Worlds*. Berkeley: University of California Press.

Berberich, C. ed. (2014). *The Bloomsbury Introduction to Popular Fiction*.G London: Bloomsbury.

Berensmeyer, I., Buelens, G., and Demoor, M. (2019). Introduction: Reconfiguring Authorship. In I. Berensmeyer, G. Buelens, and M. Demoor, eds., *The Cambridge Handbook of Literary Authorship*. Cambridge: Cambridge University Press, pp. 1–10.

Bloom, C. (2008). *Bestsellers: Popular Fiction since 1900*. Basingstoke: Palgrave Macmillan.

Bosker, B. (2018). The One Direction Fan-Fiction Novel that Became a Literary Sensation. *The Atlantic*, December. Available at: www.theatlantic.com/magazine/archive/2018/12/crowdsourcing-the-novel/573907/.

Botting, F. (2012). Bestselling Fiction: Machinery, Economy, Excess. In. D. Glover, ed., *The Cambridge Companion to Popular Fiction*. Cambridge: Cambridge University Press, pp. 159–74.

Bourdieu, P. (1993). *The Field of Cultural Production*. London: Polity.

Bradley, D. (2002). *The Making of the Victorian Novelist: Anxieties of Authorship in the Mass Market*. London: Routledge.

Brohaugh, W. (1997). *English Through the Ages*. New York: Writer's Digest Books.

Bronstein, J. L. (2015). *Mutualism*. Oxford: Oxford University Press.

Brouillette, S. (2014). *Literature and the Creative Economy*. Stanford: Stanford University Press.

Canfield, D. (2018). Is Tomi Adeyemi the new J. K. Rowling? *Entertainment Weekly*, 13 April. Available at: https://ew.com/books/2018/04/13/tomi-adeyemi-children-blood-bone-ya-profile/.

Carpenter, C. (2019). Five Questions for Tomi Adeyemi. *The Bookseller*, 22 November. Available at: www.thebookseller.com/booknews/five-questions-tomi-adeyemi-1116896.

Carras, C. and Faughnder, R. (2020). Penguin Random House to Purchase Simon & Schuster in Massive Publishing Deal. *LA Times*, 25 November. Available at: www.latimes.com/entertainment-arts/books/story/2020-11-25/penguin-random-house-buys-simon-and-schuster.

Coslor, E. (2010). Hostile Worlds and Questionable Speculation: Recognizing the Plurality of Views about Art and the Market. *Economic Action in Theory and Practice*, 30, 209–24.

Cox, C. (2016). Second-Hand Book Store Overrun with Donated Copies of *Fifty Shades of Grey* Resorts to Fortin'. *The Mary Sue*. Available at: www.themarysue.com/fifty-shades-of-grey-fort/.

Darnton, R. (1982). What is the History of Books? *Daedalus*, 111.3, 65–83.

Deahl, R. (2012). E. L. James: PW's Publishing Person of the Year. *Publishers Weekly*, 30 November. Available at: www.publishersweekly .com/pw/by-topic/industry-news/people/article/54956-e-l-james-pw-s-publishing-person-of-the-year.html.

Deahl, R. (2014). The Rise of the Seven-Figure Advance. *Publishers Weekly*, 21 November. Available at: www.publishersweekly.com/pw/ by-topic/industry-news/book-deals/article/64848-the-rise-of-the-seven-figure-advance.html.

Demetrios, H. (2019). How to Lose a Third of a Million Dollars Without Really Trying. Available at: https://forge.medium.com/how-to-lose-a-third-of-a-million-dollars-without-really-trying-d3c343675aca.

Driscoll, B. (2008). How Oprah's Book Club Reinvented the Woman Reader. *Popular Narrative Media*, 1.2, 139–50.

Driscoll, B. and Squires, C. (2020). The Epistemology of Ullapoolism: Making Mischief from within Contemporary Book Cultures. *Angelaki*, 25.5, 137–55.

Elliott, T. (2018). Markus Zusak: 'I was Just Failing and Failing, Over and Over Again'. *The Sydney Morning Herald*, 6 October. Available at: www .smh.com.au/entertainment/books/markus-zusak-i-was-just-failing-and-failing-over-and-over-again-20181001-p5071j.html.

English, J. F. and Frow, J. (2006). Literary Authorship and Celebrity Culture. In J. English, ed., *A Concise Companion to Contemporary British Fiction*. Oxford: Blackwell, pp. 39–57.

Enni, S. (2019). First Draft Episode #215: Leigh Barudgo Transcript. *First Draft*, 15 October. Available at: www.firstdraftpod.com/episode-tran scripts/2020/2/3/leigh-bardugo.

Evain, C. (2004). John Grisham's Megabestsellers. In F. Gallix and V. Guignery, eds. *Crime Fictions: Subverted Codes and New Structures*. Paris: Sorbonne PUPS, pp. 109–24.

Faktorovich, A. (2014). *The Formulas of Popular Fiction*. Jefferson, NC: McFarland.

Fisher, J. (2012). The Publishing Paradigm: Commercialism versus Creativity. In D. Hecq, ed. *The Creativity Market: Creative Writing in the 21st Century*. Bristol: Multilingual Matters, pp. 54–65.

Flood, A. (2020). First George RR Martin, now Patrick Rothfuss: The Curse of Sequel-Hungry Fans. *The Guardian*, 30 July. Available at: www.theguardian.com/books/booksblog/2020/jul/29/first-george-rr-martin-now-patrick-rothfuss-the-curse-of-sequel-hungry-fans.

Florida, R. (2002). *The Rise of the Creative Class*. New York: Basic Books.

Foucault, M. (2002). What is an Author? In W. Irwin, ed., *The Death and Resurrection of the Author*. Westport, CT: Greenwood, pp. 9–22.

Fujii, M. (2014). Haruki Murakami's 'Colorless Tsukuru' Tops Best-Seller List Again. *The Wall Street Journal*, 1 September. Available at: www.wsj.com/articles/BL-JRTB-17810.

Gabaldon, D. (2020). FAQs. Available at: www.dianagabaldon.com/resources/faq/.

Gelder, K. (2004). *Popular Fiction: The Logics and Practices of a Literary Field*. London: Routledge.

Gelder, K. ed. (2016). *New Directions in Popular Fiction: Genre, Distribution, Reproduction*. London: Palgrave Macmillan.

Gentry, B. (2018). Unstoppable: YA Fantasy Author Leigh Bardugo on World-Building and Having Faith in Your Abilities. *Writer's Digest*, 2 February. Available at: www.writersdigest.com/be-inspired/the-wd-interview-ya-fantasy-author-leigh-bardugo.

Glăveanu, V. P. (2014). *Distributed Creativity: Thinking Outside the Box of the Creative Individual*. Cham: Springer.

Glover, D. and McCracken, S. eds. (2012). *The Cambridge Companion to Popular Fiction*. Cambridge: Cambridge University Press.

Gould, E. (2014). Into the Woods. In C. Harbach, ed., *MFA vs NYC*. New York: Faber and Faber, pp. 121–37.

Grady, C. (2017). The Convoluted World of Bestseller Lists Explained. *Vox*, 13 September.

Gray, T. (2019). Robert Macfarlane and the Dark Side of Nature Writing. *The New York Times*, 28 May. Available at: www.nytimes.com/2019/05/28/books/robert-macfarlane-underland.html.

Hecq, D. ed. (2012). *The Creativity Market: Creative Writing in the 21st Century*. Bristol: Multilingual Matters.

Hennessey, C. (2018). The Secret Lives of Writers (and their Day Jobs). *The Irish Times*, 5 October. Available at: www.irishtimes.com/culture/books/the-secret-lives-of-writers-and-their-day-jobs-1.3651509.

Hentges, S. (2018). *Girls on Fire: Transformative Heroines in Young Adult Dystopian Literature*. Jefferson, NC: McFarland.

Khatchadourian, R. (2020). N. K. Jemisin's Dream Worlds. *The New Yorker*, 20 January. Available at: www.newyorker.com/magazine/2020/01/27/nk-jemisins-dream-worlds.

King, S. (2000). *On Writing: A Memoir of the Craft*. London: Hodder and Stoughton.

Kirkpatrick, D. P. (2019). Sitting at J. K. Rowling's Table. Available at: https://writingcooperative.com/sitting-at-j-k-rowlings-table-1b12eade0d4d.

KRT. (2002). J.K. Rowling: Busting the Myths. *The Age*, 28 August. Available at: www.theage.com.au/entertainment/books/j-k-rowling-busting-the-myths-20020828-gduj7q.html.

Lahire, B. (2010). The Double Life of Writers. G. Wells trans. *New Literary History*, 14.2, 443–65.

Lee, H. (2017). The Political Economy of 'Creative Industries'. *Media, Culture, and Society*, 39.7, 1078–88.

Lord, A. (2020). J. K. Rowling Shut Down and Edinburgh Cafe's Long-Held Claim that it's the Birthplace of *Harry Potter*. *The Independent*, 22 May. Available at: www.insider.com/jk-rowling-edinburgh-cafe-harry-potter-2020-5.

Magenau, J. (2018). What Makes a Book a Best-seller? *Deutsche Welle*, no date. Available at: www.dw.com/en/what-makes-a-book-a-best-seller/a-43138368.

Magner, B. (2012). Behind the BookScan Bestseller Lists: Technology and Cultural Anxieties in Early Twenty-First-Century Australia. *Script & Print*, 36.4, 243–58.

Maher, J. (2019). 'NYT' Shifts its Lists Again. *Publishers Weekly*, 26 September. Available at www.publishersweekly.com/pw/by-topic/industry-news/publisher-news/article/81272-nyt-shifts-its-lists-again.html.

MasterClass (2019). *James Patterson Teaches Writing*. Available at: www.masterclass.com/classes/james-patterson-teaches-writing.

McDowell, E. (1981). Behind the Best Sellers: Toni Morrison. *The New York Times*, 5 July. Available at: www.nytimes.com/1981/07/05/books/behind-the-best-sellers-toni-morrison.html.

McGurl, M. (2016). Everything and Less: Fiction in the Age of Amazon. *Modern Language Quarterly*, 77.3: 447–71.

Murphy, B. M. and Matterson, S. eds. (2018). *Twenty-First-Century Popular Fiction*. Edinburgh: Edinburgh University Press.

Nicolaou, E. (2018). Danielle Steel On Raising 9 Kids, Writing 174 Books, 'Authoritarian' Ex-Husbands. *Refinery 29*, 28 November. Available at: www.refinery29.com/en-us/2018/11/217825/danielle-steel-books-beauchamp-hall-successful-career-interview.

Niidas Holm, K. (2019). Q & A with Tomi Adeyemi. *Publishers Weekly*, 21 November. Available at: www.publishersweekly.com/pw/by-topic/

childrens/childrens-authors/article/81805-q-a-with-tomi-adeyemi.html.

Parlett, J. (2018). Robert Mcfarlane. *British Council*. Available at: https://literature.britishcouncil.org/writer/robert-macfarlane.

Picoult, J. (2020). FAQs. *Jodi Picoult*. Available at: www.jodipicoult.com/faqs.html.

Pierleoni, A. (2015). Best-Selling Author Dean Koontz Talks about his Success, Latest Hit Character. *The Sacramento Bee*, 2 February. Available at: www.sacbee.com/entertainment/books/article8952776.html.

Quinn, J. (1999). 'The Silence of the Lambs' Sequel Comes June 8. *Publishers Weekly*, 5 April. Available at: www.publishersweekly.com/pw/print/19990405/30649-the-silence-of-the-lambs-sequel-comes-june-8.html.

Ray Murray, P. and Squires C. (2012). The Digital Publishing Communications Circuit. *Book 2.0*, 3.1 3–23.

Reid, C. (2017). 'New York Times' Cuts a Range of Bestseller Lists. *Publishers Weekly*, 26 January. Available at www.publishersweekly.com/pw/by-topic/industry-news/comics/article/72605-new-york-times-cuts-a-range-of-bestseller-lists.html.

Reinstein, M. (2019). *Educated* Author Tara Westover Reflects on her Success, her Regrets and her Advice from Oprah. *Parade*, 6 February. Available at: https://parade.com/777230/maramovies/educated-author-tara-westover-reflects-on-her-success-her-regrets-and-her-advice-from-oprah/.

Ritz, J. (2015). Why You Should Be Reading Leigh Bardugo's Y.A. Novels – Even if You're an Adult. *Vanity Fair*, 25 September. Available at: www.vanityfair.com/culture/2015/09/leigh-bardugo-six-of-crows-grisha-trilogy-interview.

Roose, K. (2013). The Incredible Economics of *Fifty Shades of Grey*. *New York Intelligencer*, 27 March. Available at: https://nymag.com/intelligencer/2013/03/incredible-economics-of-fifty-shades.html.

Rothstein, M. (1991). A New Novel by Amy Tan, Who's Still Trying to Adapt to Success. *The New York Times*, 11 June. Available at: www.nytimes.com/1991/06/11/books/a-new-novel-by-amy-tan-who-s-still-trying-to-adapt-to-success.html.

Rowling, J. K. (2008). Text of J.K. Rowling's Speech. *The Harvard Gazette*, 5 June. Available at: https://news.harvard.edu/gazette/story/2008/06/text-of-j-k-rowling-speech/.

Sawyer, K. (2006). *Explaining Creativity*. Oxford: Oxford University Press.

Scott, A. O. (2014). The Paradox of Art as Work. *New York Times*, 11 May.

Shamsian, J. (2018). How J. K. Rowling went from Struggling Single Mom to the World's Most Successful Author. *Insider*, 31 July. Available at: www.insider.com/jk-rowling-harry-potter-author-biography-2017-7.

Smith, D. (1999). Long After 'Lambs,' Dr. Lecter is Returning. *The New York Times*, 30 March. Available at: www.nytimes.com/1999/03/30/books/long-after-lambs-dr-lecter-is-returning.html.

Smith, D. (2004). Parlaying an Affinity for Austen Into an Unexpected Best Seller. *The New York Times*, 14 June. Available at: www.nytimes.com/2004/06/14/books/parlaying-an-affinity-for-austen-into-an-unexpected-best-seller.html.

Spencer, K. (2017). Marketing and Sales in the US Young Adult Fiction Market. *New Writing*, 14.3, 429–43.

Squires, C. (2007). *Marketing Literature*. Basingstoke: Palgrave Macmillan.

Stougaard-Nielsen, J. (2019). The Author in Literary Theory and Theories of Literature. In I. Berensmeyer, G. Buelens, M. Demoor, eds., *The Cambridge Handbook of Literary Authorship*. Cambridge: Cambridge University Press, pp. 270–87.

Sullivan, J. (2015). Turning Pages: The Curse of the Big Advance for Literary Novels. *Sydney Morning Herald*, 12 December. Available at:

www.smh.com.au/entertainment/books/turning-pages-the-curse-of-the-big-advance-for-literary-novels-20151211-gllqza.html.

Sutherland, J. (1981) *Bestsellers: Popular Fiction of the 1970s*. London: Routledge and Kegan Paul.

Sutherland, J. (2007). *Bestsellers: A Very Short Introduction*. Oxford: Oxford University Press.

Tanggaard, L. (2012). The Sociomateriality of Creativity in Everyday Life. *Culture and Psychology*, 19.1, 20–32.

The Sydney Morning Herald (2002). Having a Spell. 25 May. Available at: www.smh.com.au/entertainment/books/having-a-spell-20020525-gdfb44.html.

Throsby, D. (2008). Globalization and the Cultural Economy: A Crisis of Value? In H. Anheier and R. Yudhishtir, eds., *The Cultural Economy*. London: Sage, pp. 29–41.

Velthuis, O. (2007). *Talking Prices: Symbolic Meaning of Prices on the Market for Contemporary Art*. Princeton: Princeton University Press.

Wappler, M. (2017). The Boundary-pushing Fiction of Sean McDonald and his New FSG Imprint, MCD. *Los Angeles Times*, 28 July. Available at: www.latimes.com/books/jacketcopy/la-ca-jc-mcd-imprint-20170728-story.html.

Webb, J. (2012). Creativity and the Marketplace. In D. Hecq, ed., *The Creativity Market: Creative Writing in the 21st Century*. Bristol: Multilingual Matters, pp. 40–53.

Webster, J. (2014). *The Marketplace of Attention*. Cambridge, MA: The MIT Press.

Wilkins, K. (2014). Writing Resilience in the Digital Age. *New Writing*, 11.1, 67–76.

Wilkins, K. (2017a). 'A Crowd at your Back': Fantasy Fandom and Small Press. *Media International Australia* 170.1, 115–25.

Wilkins, K. (2017b). Writing Time: Coleridge, Creativity, and Commerce. *Text*, 41.

Wilkins, K. (2019). Do the Hustle: Writing in a Post-digital Publishing World. *Sydney Review of Books*, 27 September.

Wilkins, K., Driscoll, B., and Fletcher L. (in press). *Genre Worlds: Popular Fiction in the Twenty-First Century*. Amherst: University of Massachusetts Press.

Williams, A. (2003). The New Literary Lottery. *New York Magazine*, 11 July. Available at: https://nymag.com/nymetro/news/media/features/n_8972/.

Williams, R. (1983). *Culture & Society*. New York: Columbia University Press.

Wood, H. (2019). Susanna Clarke's 'Perfectly Constructed' New Novel goes to Bloomsbury. *The Bookseller*, 30 September. Available at: www.thebookseller.com/news/susanna-clarkes-perfectly-constructed-next-novel-goes-bloomsbury-15-years-after-jonathan.

Wroe, N. (2011). A Life in Writing: John Grisham. *The Guardian*, 26 November. Available at: www.theguardian.com/culture/2011/nov/25/john-grisham-life-in-writing.

Wynne, Paula. (2020). *Pimp My Fiction: Write a Bestselling Novel by Learning Powerful Writing Techniques*. Kindle Edition. Available at: www.amazon.com/Pimp-My-Fiction-Bestselling-Techniques-ebook/dp/B0190T0Z24/.

Yucesoy, B., Wang, X., Huang, J., and Barabasi, A. (2018). Success in Books: A Big Data Approach to Bestsellers. *EPJ Data Science*, 7.7, doi.org/10.1140/epjds/s13688-018-0135-y.

Zelizer, Viviana. (2005). Circuits within Capitalism. In Nee, V. and Swedeburg, R. eds., *The Economic Sociology of Capitalism*. Princeton: Princeton University Press, pp. 289–321.

Cambridge Elements ≡

Publishing and Book Culture

SERIES EDITOR
Samantha Rayner
University College London

Samantha Rayner is a Reader in UCL's Department of
Information Studies. She is also Director of UCL's Centre for
Publishing, co-Director of the Bloomsbury CHAPTER
(Communication History, Authorship, Publishing, Textual
Editing and Reading) and co-editor of the Academic Book of
the Future BOOC (Book as Open Online Content) with UCL
Press.

ASSOCIATE EDITOR
Leah Tether
University of Bristol

Leah Tether is Professor of Medieval Literature and Publishing
at the University of Bristol. With an academic background in
medieval French and English literature and a professional
background in trade publishing, Leah has combined her
expertise and developed an international research profile in
book and publishing history from manuscript to digital.

About the series

This series aims to fill the demand for easily accessible, quality texts available for teaching and research in the diverse and dynamic fields of Publishing and Book Culture. Rigorously researched and peer-reviewed Elements will be published under themes, or 'Gatherings'. These Elements should be the first check point for researchers or students working on that area of publishing and book trade history and practice: we hope that, situated so logically at Cambridge University Press, where academic publishing in the UK began, it will develop to create an unrivalled space where these histories and practices can be investigated and preserved.

Cambridge Elements ≡

Publishing and Book Culture

Bestsellers

Gathering Editor: Beth Driscoll

Beth Driscoll is Associate Professor in Publishing and Communications at the University of Melbourne. She is the author of *The New Literary Middlebrow* (Palgrave Macmillan, 2014), and her research interests include contemporary reading and publishing, genre fiction and post-digital literary culture.

Gathering Editor: Lisa Fletcher

Lisa Fletcher is Professor of English at the University of Tasmania. Her books include *Historical Romance Fiction: Heterosexuality and Performativity* (Ashgate, 2008) and *Popular Fiction and Spatiality: Reading Genre Settings* (Palgrave Macmillan, 2016).

Gathering Editor: Kim Wilkins

Kim Wilkins is an Professor of Writing and Publishing at the University of Queensland. She is also the author of more than thirty popular fiction novels

---

ELEMENTS IN THE GATHERING

Printed in the United States
by Baker & Taylor Publisher Services